How to Get Rid of "it"

Before "it" Gets Rid of You

Topical Handbook for
Healing and Deliverance
from Spiritual Weakness

A Practical Self-Help Guide to
Spiritual and Personal Growth

A series of easy spiritual exercises, interactive tools,
And step-by-step instructions to receive
Freedom from bondage
And experience spiritual healing and deliverance

Volume Nine

ISBN-13: 978-1986460200

ISBN-10: 1986460207

How to Get Rid of "it"

Before "it" Gets Rid of You

Topical Handbook for Healing and Deliverance from Spiritual Weakness

A Practical Self-Help Guide to Spiritual and Personal Growth

A series of easy spiritual exercises, interactive tools,
And step-by-step instructions to receive
Freedom from bondage
And experience spiritual healing and deliverance

Volume Nine

Compilations of Works
By
Dr. Paulette Douglas

DEDICATION

**This book is dedicated to my Loving, Supportive, Faithful Sister,
The Late Dr. Evangelist, Rosalind Pillars**

**My God Sister (Roz) always inspires me to be the Women that God has ordained me to be
and to continue to minister to God's people and to make full proof of my ministry**

PREFACE

How to Get Rid of "it", Before "it" Gets Rid of You is a Deliverance and Spiritual Warfare Manual compiled by Dr. Paulette Douglas which is worth reading and re-reading more than once, in order to empower the reader when confronting personal crisis and trials. Dr. Paulette Douglas has compiled many practical, spiritual books bringing light to the evil that exists. She brings the deliverance ministry to the forefront, explaining how each and every believer can counteract evil and the devil. Not many believers understand the concept of the Holy Spirit and that we are all called to fight against the devil, our enemy. Dr. Paulette Douglas presents scriptural background and Bible passages from the old and new testaments, as well as prayers to share with the reader that each of us is called to resist and fight against the devil with the power of the Holy Spirit. Dr. Paulette Douglas refers to this as the deliverance ministry and explains this is one of the privileges all believers have at our disposal.

This background scripture material is necessary as many readers may be unfamiliar with these spiritual concepts. The main focus on the book is to be a manual; or one stop guide to show the reader what the bible has to say about deliverance as well as to expose the works and deceptions of the devil as well. The cover itself might seem an actual handbook- yet this book is truly a manual for deliverance. This exhaustive book contains too much information to be digested in a single, quick reading. The words contained are life changing. While some traditional readers and those in organized religion may find this book difficult to believe and a bit theatrical, a close-minded attitude is exactly what the devil wants in order to operate.

It is important to keep in mind the charismatic background of Dr. Paulette Douglas is based on the belief of the real workings of the Holy Spirit and the literal belief in modern day spiritual gifts such as tongues and healing. Much of the book is an invaluable resource where Dr. Douglas has taken scriptural truths and prayers and relates them to the modern-day believer to use and apply when facing any trial or work from the enemy. The scriptural references will empower any reader with a quick resource of how to respond in faith to any difficulty- large and small. It is a spiritual self-help book in the fact that it will allow the reader the tools to look within himself/her-self and identify any areas or issues where Satan has his foothold. Not only that it tells the reader how to face and address these issues! For those who are at a loss of how to begin to approach their spiritual problems there are a number of sample prayers applicable to any number of situations. The reader will get the impression as if this book was written for his or her own situation. This is a book to meditate on and use- and is not intended to collect dust on a book shelf. There are eleven sequels to this handbook which address many other issues that just might cover your "it".

In this twelve-book series, How to Get Rid of "it" Before "it" gets Rid of You we discuss evil spirits and how they operate:
1. The Apostolic anointing and ministry
2. How demons enter and oppress people
3. Curses and how to deal with them
4. Breaking bondages
5. Casting out spirits

6. Healing the wounded heart
7. Ungodly beliefs
8. Ministering to people
9. House cleansing
10. Discerning of spirits

In this volume we deal with the root causes of the "it' of spiritual weakness and How to get rid of the "it" of spiritual weakness before it gets rid of you. Spiritual weakness is something what plagues many people today, whether spiritual weakness is in food, sex, drugs, alcohol, smoking, spending, masturbation, porn, etc. Some inexperienced deliverance ministers might go after a spirit of spiritual weakness, which may bring freedom, but often, it doesn't bring lasting freedom. Many times, there is a root that needs to be pulled up, alongside casting out any residing spirits that are holding the person in bondage to the spiritual weakness. Getting to the root of the spiritual weakness is the key to bringing a person lasting genuine freedom. I am going to address the most common roots to spiritual weakness, and hopefully give you an idea of how this bondage works so that you can minister lasting freedom to this type of bondage.

INTRODUCTION

"It Is Finished"
The Words of Victory

"When Jesus therefore had received the vinegar, he said, "It is finished.""—John 19:30
Words of triumph. In His words, "My God, my God, why hast thou forsaken me?" we heard the Savior's cry of desolation. In His words, "I thirst" we listened to His cry of lamentation. Now there falls upon our ears His cry of jubilation— "It is finished." From the words of the victim we turn now to the words of the Victor. The Cross of Christ has two great sides to it: it showed the profound depths of His humiliation, but it also marked the goal of the Incarnation, and further, it told the consummation of His mission, and it forms the basis of our salvation.

It is finished." What is found in these three words, "It is finished" is wrapped up the Gospel of God. In these words, contained the ground of the believer's assurance. In those words, is discovered the sum of all joy, and the very spirit of all divine consolation. Every" it" that we could ever encounter in our lives was dealt with on the cross therefore; we have the victory through Jesus Christ over any and every "it".

"It is finished." This was not the despairing cry of a helpless martyr. It was not an expression of satisfaction that the termination of His sufferings was now reached. It was not the last gasp of a worn-out life. No, rather was it the declaration on the part of the divine Redeemer that all for which He came from heaven to earth to do, was now done; that all that was needed to reveal the full character of God had now been accomplished; that all that was required by the Law before sinners could be saved, had now been performed—that the full price of our redemption was now paid.

"It is finished." The great purpose of God in the history of man was now accomplished—from the beginning, God's purpose has always been one and indivisible. It had been declared to men in numerous ways: in symbol and type, by mysterious hints and by plain intimations, through Messianic prediction and through didactic declaration. That purpose of God may be summarized thus: to display His grace in the creating of children in His own image and glory. And at the Cross the foundation was laid which was to make this possible and actual.

"It is finished." What was finished? The answer to this question is a very full one, though many excellent expositors have sought to limit the scope of these words and to confine them strictly to a single application. We are told it was the prophecies concerning the sufferings of Jesus which were finished, and that He referred only to this. It is readily granted that the immediate reference was to the Messianic predictions, yet we think there are good and sufficient reasons for not confining our Lord's words here to them. Yea, to us it seems certain that Christ referred specially to His sacrificial work, for all Scripture concerning His suffering and shame was not yet fulfilled. There remained the dismissal of His spirit into the hands of the Father (Psa 31:5); there remained the "piercing" with the spear (Zec 12:10: and note that the word used in Psalm 22:16 for the piercing of His hands and feet—the act of crucifixion—is a different one); there still remained the preserving of His bones unbroken (Psa 34:20), and the burial in the rich man's grave (Isa 53:9).

"It is finished." What was finished? We answer His sacrificial work. It is true there yet remained the act of death itself, which was necessary for the making of atonement. But, as is so often the case here in John's Gospel wherein our text is found (cf. Joh 12:23, 31; 13:31; 16:5; 17:4), the Lord here speaks of the completion of His work. Moreover, it must be remembered that the three hours darkness was already past, the awful cup had already been drained, His precious blood had already been shed, the outpoured wrath of God had already been endured; and these are the primary elements in the making of propitiation. The sacrificial work of Jesus, then, was completed, excepting only the act of death which followed immediately. But, as we shall see, the completing of the sacrificial work made an end of several things.

"It is finished."
1. Here we see the accomplished fulfillment of all the prophecies which had been written of Him here He should die. This is the immediate thought of the context: "When Jesus therefore had received the vinegar, He said, It is finished" (John 19:30). Centuries beforehand, the prophets of God had described step by step the humiliation and suffering which the coming Savior should undergo. One by one these had been fulfilled, wonderfully fulfilled, fulfilled to the very letter. Had prophecy declared that He should be the "woman's seed" (Gen 3:15), then He was "born of a woman" (Gal 4:4). Had prophecy announced that His mother should be a "virgin" (Isa 7:14), then was it literally fulfilled (Mat 1:18). Had prophecy revealed that He should be of the seed of Abraham (Gen 22:18), then mark its fulfillment (Mat 1:1). Had prophecy made it known that He

Prophecy said that He should be named before He was born (Isa 49:1), then so it came to pass (Luke 1:30-31). Had prophecy foretold that He should be born in Bethlehem of Judea (Mic 5:2), then mark how this very village was His birthplace. Had prophecy forewarned that His birth should entail sorrowing for others (Jer 31:15), then behold its tragic fulfillment (Mat 2:14-18). Had prophecy foreshown that the Messiah should appear before the scepter of tribal ascendancy had departed from Judah (Gen 49:10), then so He did, for though the ten tribes were in captivity, Judah was still in the land at the time of His advent. Had prophecy referred to the flight into Egypt and the subsequent return into Palestine, (Hose 11:1 and cf. Isa 49:3, 6), then so it came to pass (Mat 2:1415).

Prophecy made mention of one going before Christ to make ready His way (Mal 3:1), then see its fulfillment in the person of John the Baptist. Had prophecy made it known that at the Messiah's appearing "the eyes of the blind shall be opened, and the ears of the deaf shall be unstopped, then shall the lame man leap as a hart, and the tongue of the dumb sing" (Isa 35:56), then read through the four Gospels and see how blessedly this proved true. Had prophecy spoken of Him as "poor and needy" (Psa 40:17, see beginning of Psalm), then behold Him not having where to lay His head. Had prophecy intimated that He should speak in "parables" (Psa 78:2), then such was frequently His method of teaching. Had prophecy depicted Him stilling the tempest (Psa 107:29), then this is exactly what He did. Had prophecy heralded His "triumphal entry" into Jerusalem (Zec 9:9), then so it came to pass!

Prophecy announced that His person should be despised (Isa 53:3), that He should be rejected by the Jews (Isa 8:14), that He should be "hated without a cause" (Psa 69:4), then sad to say, such was precisely the case. Had prophecy painted the whole picture of His degradation and crucifixion, then was it vividly reproduced. There had been the betrayal by a familiar friend, the forsaking by His disciples, the being led to the slaughter, the being taken to judgment, the appearing of false witnesses against Him, the refusal on His part to make defense, the establishing of His innocence, the unjust condemnation, the sentence of capital punishment passed upon Him, the literal piercing of His hands and feet, the being numbered with transgressors, the mockery of the crowd, the casting lots for His garments—all predicted centuries beforehand, and all fulfilled to the very letter. The last prophecy of all which remained here He committed His Spirit into the hands of His Father, had now been fulfilled. He cried "I thirst," and after the tendering of the vinegar and gall, all was now "accomplished"; and as the Lord Jesus reviewed the entire scope of the prophetic Word and saw its full realization, He cried,

"It is finished"!
It only remains for us to point out that as there was a complete set of prophecies which had to do with the first advent of Jesus, so also is there a complete set of prophecies which have to do with His second advent—the latter as definite, as personal, and as comprehensive in their scope as the former. As then we see the actual fulfillment of those which had to do with His first coming to the earth, we may look forward with absolute confidence and assurance to the fulfillment of those which have to do with His second coming. And, as we have seen that the former set of prophecies were fulfilled literally and personally, so also must we expect the latter set to be. To grant the literal fulfillment of the former, and then to seek to spiritualize and symbolize the latter, is not only grossly inconsistent and illogical, but is highly injurious to us and deeply dishonoring to God and to His Word.

"It is finished."
2. Here we see the completion of His sufferings. But what tongue or pen can describe the sufferings of Jesus? The anguish, physical, mental, and spiritual, which He endured! Appropriately was He designated "the man of sorrows": suffering at the hands of men, at the hands of Satan, and at the hands of God. Pain inflicted upon Him by enemies and friends alike. From the beginning He walked the shadows which the Cross cast His path. "I am afflicted and ready to die from my youth up" (Psa 88:15). What a light this throws on His earlier years! Who can say how much is contained in those words? For us, an impenetrable veil is cast over the future; none of us knows what a day may bring forth.

But Jesus knew the end from the beginning! One has only to read through the Gospels to learn how the awful Cross was ever before Him. At the marriage-feast of Cana, where all was gladness and merriment, He makes solemn reference to "his hour" not yet come. When Nicodemus interviewed Him at night, the Savior referred to the "lifting up of the Son of man." When James and John came to request from Him the two places of honor in His coming kingdom, He made mention of the "cup" which He had to drink, and of the "baptism" wherewith He must be baptized. When Peter confessed that He was the Christ, the Son of the living God, He turned to His disciples and began to show unto them "how that he must go unto Jerusalem, and suffer many things of the elders and chief priests and scribes, and be killed, and be raised again the third day" (Mat 16:21). When Moses and Elijah stood with Him on the Mount of Transfiguration, it was to speak of "his decease which he should accomplish at Jerusalem" (Luke 9:31).

If it is true we are quite unable to estimate the sufferings of Christ due to the anticipation of the Cross, still less can we fathom the dread reality itself. The physical sufferings were excruciating, but even this was as nothing compared with His anguish of soul. To a consideration of these sufferings we have already devoted several paragraphs in previous chapters, yet we make no apology in turning to them again. We cannot contemplate too often what Jesus endured to secure our salvation. The better we are acquainted with His sufferings, and the more frequently we meditate thereon, the warmer will be our love and the deeper our gratitude.
At last the closing hours have come. There had been the terrible experience in Gethsemane followed by the appearing before Caiaphas, before Pilate, before Herod, and back again before Pilate. There had been the scourging and mocking by the brutal soldiers; the journey to Calvary; the fastening of His hands and feet to the cruel tree. There had been the reviling of the priests, the crowd, and the two thieves crucified with Him.

There had been the awful cloud that hid from the Father's face, which wrung from Him the bitter cry, "My God, my God, why hast thou forsaken me?" There had been the parched lips which drew from Him the exclamation "I thirst." There had been the fearful conflict with the power of darkness as the serpent "bruised" His heel. But now the suffering is ended. The Lord has bruised Him; man, and Devil have done their worst. The cup has been drained. The awful storm of God's wrath has spent itself. The darkness is ended. The sword of divine justice is done. The wages of sin have been paid. The prophecies of His sufferings are all fulfilled. The Cross has been "endured." Divine holiness has been fully satisfied (Isa 53:11). With a cry of triumph—a loud cry, a cry which reverberated throughout the entire universe—Jesus exclaims, "It is finished." The shame, the suffering and agony, are past. Never again shall He experience pain. Never again shall He endure the contradiction of sinners against Himself. Never again shall He be in the hands of Satan. Never again shall the light of God's countenance be hidden from Him. Blessed be God, all that is finished! "It is finished."

Jesus is concerned in the work of Redemption: He was the One who came here to die for sinners. He is the One who now gives spiritual illumination and understanding, and guides into the truth. Before the Lord Jesus came to this earth, a definite work was committed to Him. In the volume of the book it was written of Him, and He came to do the recorded will of God. Even as a boy of twelve the "Father's business" was before His heart and occupied His attention. Again, in John 5:36 we find Him saying, "But I have greater witness than that of John: for the works which the Father hath given me to finish, the same works that I do." And on the last night before His death, in that wonderful high priestly prayer, we find Him saying, "I have glorified thee on the earth: I have finished the work which thou gavest me to do" (John 17:4).

The mission upon which God had sent His Son into the world was now accomplished. It was not actually finished till He breathed His last, but death was only an instant ahead, and in anticipation of it He cries "It is finished." The demanding work is done. The divinely-given task is performed. A work more honorable and momentous than ever entrusted to man or angels, has been completed. That for which He had left heaven's glory that for which He had taken upon Him the form of a servant, that for which He had remained upon earth for thirty-three years to do, was now consummated. Nothing remained to be added. The goal of the Incarnation is reached. With what joyous triumph must He here have viewed the costly work which, committed to Him, had now been perfected!

"It is finished." The mission upon which God had sent His Son into the world was accomplished. That which had been eternally purposed had come to pass. The plan of God had been fully carried out.

Because He is the Most High, God's will, cannot be thwarted. Because He is supreme, God's counsel must stand. Because He is almighty, God's purpose cannot be overthrown.

"But he is in one mind, and who can turn him? And what his soul desireth, even that he doeth" (Job 23:13). "I know that thou canst do everything, and that no thought can be withholding from thee" (Job 42:2). "But our God is in the heavens: He hath done whatsoever he hath pleased" (Psa 115:3). "There is no wisdom nor understanding nor counsel against the Lord" (Pro 21:30). "For the Lord of hosts hath purposed, and who shall disannul it? And His hand is stretched out, and who shall turn it back?" (Isa 14:27). "Remember the former things of old: for I am God, and there is none else; I am God, and there is none like me: Declaring the end from the beginning, and from ancient times the things that are not yet done, saying, My counsel shall stand, and I will do all my pleasure" (Isa 46:9-10). "And all the inhabitants of the earth are reputed as nothing: and he doeth according to his will in the army of heaven, and among the inhabitants of the earth: and none can stay his hand, or say unto him, What doest thou?" (Dan 4:35). And, in the triumphant cry of the Jesus— "It is finished"—we have a prophecy and pledge of the ultimate carrying out of God's plan completely. At the end of time, when everything is wound up, and God's purpose has been fully consummated, when everything has been done which He before determined should be done, then shall it be said again, "It is finished."

"It is finished."

4. Here we see the accomplishment of the Atonement. Above we have spoken of Christ reaching the goal of the Incarnation, and of the consummation of His mission to the earth; what that goal and mission was, the Scriptures plainly reveal. The Son of Man came here "to seek and to save that which was lost" (Luke 19:10). Christ Jesus came into the world "to save sinners" (1Ti 1:15). God sent forth His Son, born of a woman, "to redeem them that were under the law" (Gal 4:5). He was manifested "to take away our sins" (1Jo 3:5). And all this involved the Cross. The "lost" which He came to seek could only be found there—in the place of death and under the condemnation of God. Sinners could be "saved" only by One taking their place and bearing their iniquities. They who were under the Law could be "redeemed" only by Another fulfilling its requirements and suffering its curse. Our sins could be "taken away" only by their being blotted out by the precious blood of Christ. The demands of justice must be met; the requirements of God's holiness must be satisfied; the awful debt we incurred must be paid. And on the Cross, this was done; done by none less than the Son of God; done perfectly; done once for all.

"It is finished."

That to which so many types looked forward, was now accomplished. A covering from sin and its shame, typified by the coats of skin with which the Lord God clothed our first parents, was now provided. The more excellent sacrifice, typified by Abel's lamb, had now been offered. A shelter from the storm of divine judgment, typified by the Ark of Noah, was now furnished. The only-begotten and well-beloved Son, typified by Abraham's offering up of Isaac, had already been placed upon the altar. A protection from the avenging angel, typified by the shed blood of the Passover-lamb, was now supplied. A cure from the serpent's bite, typified by the serpent of brass upon the pole, was now made ready for sinners. The providing of a life-giving fountain, typified by Moses striking the rock, was now affected.

"It is finished." The Greek word here, teleo, is translated variously in the New Testament. A glance at some of the different renderings in other passages will enable us to discern the fullness and finality of the term used by Jesus. In Matthew 11:1, teleo is rendered as follows, "When Jesus had made an end of commanding his twelve disciples, he departed thence." In Matthew 17:24 it is rendered, "They that received tribute money came to Peter, and said, Doth not your master pay tribute?" In Luke 2:39, it is rendered, "And when they had performed all things according to the Law of the Lord, they returned into Galilee." In Luke 18:31, it is rendered, "All things that are written by the prophets concerning the Son shall be accomplished."

"It is finished." He cried: it is "made an end of"; it is "paid"; it is "performed"; it is "accomplished." What was made an end of? —our sins and their guilt. What was "paid?"—the price of our redemption. What was "performed?"—the utmost requirements of the Law. What was "accomplished?"—the work which the Father had given Him to do. What was "finished?"— the making of atonement. God has furnished at least four proofs that Christ did finish the work which was given Him to do. First, in the rending of the veil, which showed that the way to God was now open. Second, in the raising of Christ from the dead, which evidenced that God had accepted His sacrifice. Third, the exaltation of Christ to His own right hand, which demonstrated the value of Christ's work and the Father's delight in His person. Fourth, the sending to earth of the Holy Spirit to apply the virtues and benefits of Christ's atoning death.

"It is finished." What was "finished?"—the work of atonement. What is the value of that to us? This: to the sinner, it is a message of glad tidings. All that a Holy God requires has been done. Nothing is left for the sinner to add. No works from us are demanded as the price of our salvation. All that is necessary for the sinner is to rest now by faith upon what Christ did. "The gift of God is eternal life through Jesus Christ our Lord" (Rom 6:23). To the believer, the knowledge that the atoning work of Christ is finished brings a sweet relief over against all the defects and imperfections of his services. There is nothing "finished" that we do: all our duties are imperfect. There is much of sin and vanity in the very best of our efforts, but the grand relief is that we are "complete" in Christ (Col 2:10)! Christ and His finished work are the ground of all our hopes. "It is finished."

5. Here we see the end of our sins. The sins of the believer, all of them, were transferred to the Jesus. As the Scripture says, "The Lord hath laid on him the iniquities of us all" (Isa 53:6). If then God laid my iniquities on Christ, they are no longer on me. Sin there is in me, for the old Adamic nature remains in the believer till death or till Christ's return, should He come before I die; but there is no sin on me. This distinction between sin in and sin on, is a vital one, and there should be little difficulty in apprehending it. If I were to say the judge passed sentence on a criminal, and that he is now under sentence of death, everyone would understand what I meant. In like manner, everyone out of Christ has the sentence of God's condemnation resting upon him. But when a sinner believes in the Lord Jesus, and receives Him as his Lord and Master, obey the salvation message according to (Acts 2:38-39) he is no longer "under condemnation"— sin is no longer on him, that is, the guilt, the condemnation, the penalty of sin, is no longer upon

him. And why? Because Christ bore our sins in His own body on the tree (1Pe 2:24)—the guilt, condemnation, and penalty of our sins, was transferred to our substitute. Hence, because my sins were transferred to Christ, they are no more upon me.

This precious truth was strikingly illustrated in Old Testament times regarding Israel's annual Day of Atonement. On that day, Aaron, the high priest (a type of Christ), made satisfaction to God for the sins which Israel had committed during the previous year. The way this was done is described in Leviticus 16. Two goats were taken and presented before the Lord at the door of the tabernacle: this was before anything was done with them: it represented Christ being sent and presenting Himself, offering to come into this world and be the Savior of sinners. One of the goats was then taken and killed, and its blood was carried into the tabernacle, within the veil, into the Holy of Holies, and there it was sprinkled before and upon the mercy seat—foreshadowing Christ offering Himself as a sacrifice, to meet the demands of His justice and satisfy the requirements of His holiness.

Then we read that Aaron came out of the tabernacle and laid both his hands upon the head of the second (living) goat— signifying an act of identification by which Aaron is the representative of the whole nation, identified the people with it, acknowledging that its doom was what their sins merited, and which, today, corresponds with the hands of faith laying hold of Christ and identifying ourselves with Him in His Death. Having laid his hands on the head of the live goat, Aaron now confessed over him "all the iniquities of the children of Israel, and all their transgressions in all their sins, putting them upon the head of the goat" (Lev 16:21). Thus, were Israel's sins transferred to their substitute. Finally, we are told, "And the goat shall bear upon him all their iniquities unto a land not inhabited: and he shall let go the goat in the wilderness" (Lev 16:22). The goat bearing Israel's sins, was taken unto an uninhabited wilderness, and the people of God saw him and their sins no more! In type this was Christ taking our sins into that desolate land where God was not and there making an end of them. The Cross of Christ then is the grave of our sins!

"It is finished."
6. Here we see the fulfillment of the Law's requirements. "The law is holy, and the commandment holy, and just and good" (Rom 7:12). How could it be anything less when Jehovah Himself had framed and given it! The fault lay not in the Law but in man who, being depraved and sinful, could not keep it. Yet that Law must be kept, and kept by a man, so that the Law might be honored and magnified, and its giver vindicated. Therefore, we read, "For what the law could not do, in that it was weak through the flesh, God sending his own Son, in the likeness of sinful flesh, and for sin, condemned sin in the flesh: that the righteousness of the law might be fulfilled in [not by] us, who walk not after flesh, but after the Spirit" (Rom 8:3-4). The "weakness" here is that of fallen man. The sending forth of God's Son in the likeness of sin's flesh (Greek) refers to the Incarnation: as we read in another Scripture, "God sent forth his Son, born of a woman, born under the law, that he might redeem them that were under the law" (Gal 4:4-5 RV). Yes, the Jesus was born "under the law," born under it that He might keep it perfectly in thought, word, and deed. "Think not that I am come to destroy the law, or the prophets: I am not come to destroy, but to fulfill" (Mat 5:17); such was His claim.

But not only did Jesus keep the precepts of the Law, He also suffered its penalty and endured its curse. We had broken it, and taking our place, He must receive its just sentence. Having received its penalty and endured its curse, the demands of the Law are fully met, and justice is satisfied. Therefore, is it written of believers, "Christ hath redeemed us from the curse of the law, being made a curse for us" (Gal 3:13). And again, "For Christ is the end of the law for righteousness to everyone that believeth" (Rom 10:4). And yet again, "For ye are not under the law, but under grace" (Rom 6:14). "It is finished." "Free from the Law, Jesus hath bled, and there is remission, cursed by the law and bruised by the fall, Grace hath redeemed us once for all."

7. Here we see the destruction of Satan's power. See it by faith. The Cross sounded the death of the devil's power. To human appearances it looked like the moment of his greatest triumph, yet, it was the hour of his ultimate defeat. In view of the Cross Jesus declared, "Now is the judgment of this world: now shall the prince of this world be cast out" (Joh 12:31). It is true that Satan has not yet been chained and cast into the bottomless pit, nevertheless, sentence has been passed (though not yet executed); his doom is certain; and his power is already broken so far as believers are concerned.

For the Christian, the devil is a vanquished foe. He was defeated by Christ at the Cross— "that through death he might destroy him that had the power of death, that is, the devil" (Hebrew 2:14). Believers have already been "delivered from the power of darkness" and translated into the kingdom of God's dear Son (Col 1:13). Satan, then, should be treated as a defeated enemy. No longer has he any legitimate claim upon us. Once we were his lawful "captives"; but now God worketh in us both to will and to do of His good pleasure. All that we now must do is to "resist the devil," and the promise is, "he will flee from you" (James 4:7).

"It is finished." Here was the triumphant answer to the rage of man and the enmity of Satan. It tells of the perfect work which meets sin in the place of judgment. All was completed just as God would have it, just as the prophets had foretold, just as the Old Testament ceremonial had foreshadowed, just as divine holiness demanded, and just as sinners needed. How strikingly appropriate is this sixth Cross-utterance of Jesus found in John's Gospel—the Gospel which displays the glory of Christ's deity! He seals it with His own words, attesting it is complete, and giving it the all-sufficient sanction of His own approval. Jesus says, "It is finished"—who then dare doubt or question it.

"It is finished." Reader, do you believe it? or, are you trying to add something of your own to the finished work of Christ to secure the favor of God? All you must do is to accept the pardon which He purchased. God is satisfied with His work on the cross, why are not you? Sinner, the moment you believe Jesus' testimony that it is finished, that moment every sin you have committed is blotted out, and you stand accepted in Christ! O would you not like to possess the assurance that there is nothing between your soul and God? Would you not like to know that every sin had been atoned for and put away? Then believe what God's Word says about Christ's death. Rest not on your feelings and experiences but on the written Word. There is only one way of finding peace, deliverance, wholeness, salvation, victory over the "it" and that is through faith in the shed blood of Jesus the of Lamb God. It is time to "Get Rid of "it", Before "it" Gets Rid of You".

"It is finished." Do you really believe it? Or, are you endeavoring to add something of your own to it and thus merit the favor of God? By continuing to hold on and struggle, seeking other sources to deal with the "it" in your life, you are nullifying the finished work of Christ by your own miserable additions to it!". The Gospel of God's grace, and the finished work of Christ is sufficient for our souls to rest upon. In the pages of this book, God uses forceful object lessons and His Word to show you, "How to Get Rid of "it", before "it" Gets Rid of You". It is a grave mistake not to embrace the Word of God, and cast yourself by faith upon what Christ had done for you.

Victory was given to us by way of the cross. Whatever your "it" or "its" might be, "it" has come to kill, steal and destroy you. Make a conscious effort to explore this information given in this book and expose the enemy of your soul. Let's "Get Rid of "it". After all, "It is Finished"

CHAPTER ONE

What is "it"?

We are all created with a basic need to be loved. God created us to both give and receive love, but though damaged emotions, our capacity to receive love can be dramatically hindered. Ignorance of God's love will also hinder us from receiving the great and glorious love that He has for us. **The root of most "its" is a lack of love being received by that person.** Many of us have been damaged emotionally by rejection, abandonment, abuse, etc., and thereby our capacity to receive love has been reduced. **Only an emotionally healthy person is capable of both giving and receiving love as God intended.**

Self-worth issues can hinder love

Self-worth issues are rooted in believing that we are not worthy or deserve to be loved. When we believe that we are unlovable, we will unconsciously reject any love that comes our way. We won't believe the love, because we believe in our hearts that we are not worthy. **Self-worth issues are all rooted in our failing to see who we really are in Christ.**

If you walked into a gallery of world-class art, and pointed to a painting, saying, "That is the ugliest thing I've ever seen! Who painted that??" Now let's say the artist was standing right next to you. How do you think that would make him feel? Do you realize we are the artwork of God, a special painting crafted together by the master painter? Do you think it brings Him honor when we look down on ourselves? **We need to stop putting down what God has made.**

Many times, we have self-unforgiveness issues because we blame ourselves for something, or we've done something we deeply regret, and we simply cannot let it go. We need to realize that Jesus has forgiven us of all our failures, and we need to start seeing ourselves as forgiven. Otherwise, we're denying the work of Christ in our life! **If God forgave you, and you're still beating yourself up, then you don't really believe what Jesus did for you.** It's that simple!

Just as we must forgive others (see Matthew 18:21-35), we need to forgive ourselves just the same. Self-hate has been known to be the root behind diseases such as lupus and Crohn's disease, as well as other auto-immune diseases. We need to stop holding ourselves accountable for that which Jesus has set us free from.

If we want to be in faith, we need to BELIEVE what Jesus did for us, and part of that believing is seeing ourselves as forgiven and clothed with the righteousness of God, which is upon all who believe in the finished work of Christ. Without faith, it is impossible to please God (see Hebrews 11:6), so if you want to please God, start taking the finished work of the cross seriously, and begin to see yourself as forgiven, washed clean, and clothed in the righteousness of God. For the righteousness (right standing with God) is upon all who believe:

> *"Even the righteousness of God which is by faith of Jesus Christ unto all and upon all them that believe..." (Romans 3:22 KJV)*

Unforgiveness is rooted in a lack of realization of how much God has forgiven us, and therefore we're not thankful for the steep and terrible price that Jesus paid for our own failures. Therefore, it is so important to mediate on what Jesus did for us, until it transforms our heart. The message of Jesus' work for us is what causes faith to arise in our hearts and transforms us from the inside out (read Romans 10:8-17).

Learning to see yourself as God sees you, and forgive yourself because you want to please God and be in faith and be thankful for what Jesus did for you, is the biggest step in overcoming self-worth issues. Of course, there are spirits that may need to be driven out as well, such as self-hate, guilt, condemnation, etc.

Receiving the love God has for us

When it comes to God's love for us, that's obvious, considering how He loves even the sinner so much that Jesus came to die for them. Anybody who knows the message of the cross, has some knowledge of God's love for us. However, many times, we blame God for our problems, and so we don't believe the love that He has for us. Not only do we blame Him for our problems, many times we think that God gave us the sickness or problem in our life to teach us something. Nothing could be further from the truth! Jesus tells us clearly who came to kill, steal, and destroy, and who came so that we could have life and have it in abundance.

> *"The thief cometh not, but for to steal, and to kill, and to destroy: I am come that they might have life, and that they might have it more abundantly." (John 10:10 KJV)*

If we are going to receive the love that God has for us, we need to get our thinking straightened out. He's not the one behind our problems, but rather Jesus paid the full price so that we can be forgiven all our sins, both physically and emotionally healed, and blessed.

> *"When the even was come, they brought unto him many that were possessed with devils: and he cast out the spirits with his word, and healed all that were*

Look at how good God's heart is toward mankind! Not only did Jesus heal them, but He proved the blessings of the covenant we have with Him today concerning our healing and deliverance. Isn't He good toward us? **The reason why things happen to us, is because we live in a fallen world that is under the control of the evil one.** <u>It's not God's fault. He loves you. Jesus died for you.</u>

Settling the fact that God loves you and is good toward you is crucial to restoring your God-given capacity to receive His love. If you can't receive His love, then you need to stop and ask yourself four questions:

1. Am I blaming God for anything bad that happened to me?

2. Have I been emotionally wounded in such a way that it is hindering my ability to freely receive love as God intended me to?

3. Do I have knowledge and revelation of how much God loves me? Do I have a solid Biblical understanding of how I am loved with the same kind of love that the Father has for Jesus?

4. Is there a self-worth issue that makes me feel unworthy to be loved?

Settling these issues lays a foundation for breaking free from the power of the "IT". You must repair the damage and faulty thinking which hinders your ability to receive the love that God has for you.

How do you know if you are receiving God's love or if it's hindered? **If you are not passionate about Jesus, then somewhere your ability to receive His love is hindered.**

If you are living a life without receiving God's love in your heart daily, you are missing out on the most fulfilling life you can have here on this earth. To know God's love, which surpasses all understanding (see Philippians 4:7), dispels all our fears and gives us a sense of peace and joy that we could never otherwise know.

What exactly is "it'?

An "it" is formed when we try to use something other than God, to meet our need to be loved. When our ability to receive God's love into our hearts is hindered, we will feel like something is missing, and seek to fill that void with something else. When that thing, whatever it might be, fills that void, we grow to love "it" because it's meeting a need. Over time, we establish a relationship with that thing, and when it comes time to depart, it's like breaking up a relationship. That's why the "it" is so destructive; we've relied on that thing to meet a need and we've established a relationship with it. Now when it's time to break up the love, it isn't so easy to say goodbye.

One widespread problem that we see when we try to deal with "it", is where we give up one "it" successfully, only to find yourself with another "it". We might quit drinking only to start overeating, for example. We might think we're finding victory, but all we're really doing is trading one "it" for another "it". This is because something must fill the love-void in our hearts, and if it's not one thing, it will be another.

What about cutting or self-harm?

Cutting or self-mutation is a special type of "it", where there's a need to either release pain in a person's heart or the person believes that they deserve to be punished for their failures. In these cases, the person certainly has an issue receiving the love that God has for them but there's another type of root that needs to be addressed as well. There's emotional pain or guilt that the person is dealing with that needs to be resolved. Finding out what happened and receiving Christ's truth concerning those areas is important for their healing. Any bondage involving guilt will need to be resolved through realizing and accepting the work of Christ on the cross for that person and they will likely need spirits of guilt, condemnation, self-hate, etc. driven out in Jesus' name. Again, getting the person to see them self for who they really are in Christ, forgiven, loved, and blessed, is crucial to lasting freedom from self-hate issues.

See yourself as lovable!

The key in uprooting most "its" is to deal with the underlying issues which are limiting their capacity to freely receive love from God and others, along with dealing with any self-worth issues by establishing an understanding of your true identity in Christ. **Coming to a place where you believe you are lovable is key to receiving love in general**, so dealing with self-worth issues is an important key to breaking down the walls which keep us from feeling loved. The only way to obtain a true sense of worth and value is to get a revelation of how much you are loved by God, who sent His son Jesus to die for you.

Discovering the root

To discover the root of your "it", you need to get real honest with yourself. Many times, we are in denial about the pain we are feeling. Figuring out what is the root of a bondage is all about asking the right questions, and that is especially important when it comes to uprooting an "it". Why don't we feel loved? Do we feel unlovable? (Let's stop right there; if we feel unlovable, then you've just discovered a self-worth issue that will need to be addressed.) Are you passionate about Jesus? If not, then something in hindering you from realizing how much you are loved by Him who died for you. Do you see yourself as forgiven and loved by the God because of what He did for you?

As you discover emotional wounds, you'll need to forgive (others, yourself, and God) and invite Jesus to come and heal the damage in your heart. If you don't realize how much God loves you, then you'll need to spend some time learning about what Jesus did for you on the cross, and what a terrible price He paid because He loved you so very much. Often breaking out of an "it" is a combination of emotional healing, learning about who you are in Christ, forgiving (yourself, others, and God), overcoming self-worth issues by changing how you see yourself (in light of how God sees and loves you), and casting out any spirits that came in and are enforcing the destructive behavior. Spirits behind guilt, condemnation, etc. also need to be driven out, as they seek to keep us from fully seeing what Jesus did for us on the cross.

Dealing with the issues underlying an "it" is key to uprooting it permanently. If you want lasting freedom and wholeness in this area of your life, you will have to deal with the issues that have limited your capacity to receive love, especially the love that God has for you.

CHAPTER TWO

The "it" of Lack of Prayer

DEFINITION: Prayer is talking to God and with God, whether it be spoken or silent conversation. Prayer is a direct line to Heaven, allowing you to communicate with God. It includes praise and worship, petition, confession, repentance, and intercession.

FACTS ABOUT PRAYER:

The greatest prayer. The greatest prayer is the prayer asking forgiveness for sin and accepting Christ as Savior (Luke 18:13).

Prayer is described as calling upon the name of the Lord (Genesis 12:8); crying unto God (Psalms 27:7; 34:6); drawing near to God (Psalms 73:28; Hebrews 10:22); looking up (Psalms 5:3); lifting up the soul (Psalms 25:1); lifting up the heart (Lamentations 3:41); pouring out the heart (Psalms 62:8); pouring out the soul (1 Samuel 1:15); crying to Heaven (2 Chronicles 32:20); beseeching the Lord (Exodus 32:11); seeking God (Job 8:5); seeking the face of the Lord (Psalms 27:8); making supplication (Job 8:5; Jeremiah 36:7).

There are three levels of intensity in prayer. Asking, seeking, and knocking (Matthew 7:7-8). Asking is the first level of prayer. It is simply presenting a request to God and receiving an immediate answer. Seeking is a deeper level of prayer where answers are not as immediate as at the asking level. Knocking is prayer that persists when answers are longer in coming.

Believers have great power in prayer. Through prayer, you have power over the enemy (Luke 9:1); power over sin (John 20:23); power to extend the gospel (Matthew 9:37); and power to bind and loose spiritual forces (Matthew 12:28-29; 16:19). Your prayers are powerful because of the name of Jesus (John 16:23-24) and His blood that secured your victory (Hebrews 10:19-23).

The Bible reveals that prayer is answered immediately at times (Isaiah 65:24; Daniel 9:21-23); delayed at times (Luke 18:7); different from your desires (2 Corinthians 12:8-9); and beyond your expectations (Jeremiah 33:3; Ephesians 3:20).

Organizing for prayer. Prayer can be made on an individual basis (Matthew 6:6); with two people praying together (Matthew 18:19); and in small groups (Matthew 18:20).

DEALING WITH PRAYER:

Never condemn a person or feel condemned for lack of prayer. Prayer is a wonderful opportunity, not an obligation that must be fulfilled. View prayer as something you might be missing rather than something you should be doing. It is not a burden, but an opportunity.

Set a special time and place to pray to God each day. You can pray anytime as you go throughout the day--and you should--but you should also have a set time and place to devote yourself solely to prayer. You plan for dinner, recreation, work, and others things. Plan for prayer!

Open your heart to receive God's guidance when you pray. Let Him know that you want to change, and invite Him to guide you in living a Spirit-filled life and being a better person. Give thanks for both good and bad circumstances in your life, as both carry lessons to teach you the right and wrong ways to approach life. Use your prayer time to ask God for help and to give thanks, confess your sins, and seek comfort and guidance.

Use the model prayer in Mathew 6:9-13 as a format for your prayer. Each phrase can be used as an outline point through which you can worship God, pray for His Kingdom around the world, pray that His will be done in your life and the lives of others, ask for and extend forgiveness, ask for provision in every area of life, and intercede for protection from temptation and the evil powers of Satan. The prayer includes an appeal for "daily bread", so it assumes that you will talk to God each day on a regular basis.

Listen for God to speak to you Prayer is communication, and a one-way conversation does not last long. When you pray, expect God to speak to you. Most often He will do this through His written Word or by a "still small voice" that seems to speak to your heart. Sometimes He will give you a vision, a prophetic word, or interpret back to your spirit what you have prayed in your heavenly prayer language.

Align your life with the purposes and priorities of God. Pray for wisdom concerning every area of your life and the forthcoming day (James 4:2).   God will show you the things that need to be done and how to do things better. He will help you discern what is and is not important, and how to use your time to accomplish His priorities and purposes.

WHAT GOD'S WORD SAYS ABOUT PRAYER:

Biblical guidelines for prayer. Study the following references in your Bible.

-Prayer is to be made to God:	Psalms 5:2
-Quality rather than quantity is stressed:	Matthew 6:7
-Empty repetition is forbidden, but sincere repetition is not:	Daniel 6:10; Luke 11:5-13; 18:1-8
-Pray with understanding (in a known tongue):	Ephesians 6:18
-Pray in the Spirit in tongues:	Romans 8:26; Jude 20
-Intercede according to the will of God:	1 John 5:14-15
-Pray in secret:	Matthew 6:6
-Pray always:	Luke 21:36; Ephesians 6:18
-Pray continually without ceasing:	Romans 12:12; 1 Thessalonians 5:17
-Intercede to the Father in the name of Jesus:	John 14:13-14
-Pray with a watchful attitude:	1 Peter 4:7
-Pray using the example of the model prayer:	Matthew 6:9-13
-Pray with a forgiving spirit:	Mark 11:25
-Pray with humility:	Matthew 6:7
-Accompany prayer with fasting:	Matthew 17:21
-Intercede fervently:	James 5:16; Colossians 4:12

-Pray with submission to God: Luke 22:42
-Use the strategies of binding and loosing: Matthew 16:19

What to pray for. Study the following Biblical references which reveal what you are to intercede for:

-The peace of Jerusalem: Psalms 122:6
-Laborers in the harvest: Matthew 9:38; Luke 10:2
-That you enter not into temptation: Luke 22:40-46;
-Those who despitefully use you (your enemies):   Luke 6:28
-All the saints: Ephesians 6:18
-The sick: James 5:14
-For others (bearing others burdens):   James 5:16;1 Samuel 12:23
-For all men, kings, and those in authority: 1 Timothy 2:1-4
-For daily needs: Matthew 6:11
-For wisdom: James 1:5
-For healing: James 5:14-15
-For forgiveness: Matthew 6:12
-For God's will and Kingdom to be established: Matthew 6:10
-For relief from affliction: James 5:13
-For unity in the Body of Christ: John 17
-For the persecuted church around the world: Hebrews 13:3

Hindrances to effective prayer. Identifying hindrances to your prayer life is not enough. You must also ask God to help you to eliminate them. Also remember that what seems to be unanswered prayer does not mean there are spiritual hindrances in your prayer life. Answers to prayer may be delayed (Luke 18:7) or answered differently from your desires (2 Corinthians 12:8-9). Here are some common hindrances to effective prayer.

-Sin of any kind: Isaiah 59:1-2; Psalm 66:18;
                                                                 Isaiah 1:15; Proverbs 28:9
-Idols in the heart: Ezekiel 14:1-3
-An unforgiving spirit: Mark 11:25; Matthew 5:23
-Selfishness, wrong motives:
        Proverbs 21:13; James 4:3
-Power hungry, manipulative prayers: James 4:2-3
-Wrong treatment of marriage partner: 1 Peter 3:7
-Self-righteousness: Luke 18:10-14
-Unbelief: James 1:6-7
-Not abiding in Christ and His Word: John 15:7
-Lack of compassion: Proverbs 21:13
-Hypocrisy, pride, meaningless repetition: Matthew 6:5; Job 35:12-13
-Not asking according to the will of God: James 4:2-3
-Not asking in Jesus' name: John 16:24
-Satanic demonic hindrances: Daniel 10:10-13; Ephesians 6:12
-Not seeking first the Kingdom: Matthew 6:33

When you don't know how to pray, allow the Holy Spirit pray through you: Romans 8:26

Study Christ's prayer for you. John 17

CHAPTER THREE

The "it" of Lack of Fasting

DEFINITION: Fasting is the willing abstinence from or the reduction of food, drink, or both for a period of time.

FACTS ABOUT FASTING:

The purpose of fasting. Fasting does not change God. It changes you. God relates to you on the basis of your relationship to Him. When you change, then the way God deals with you is affected. Read the book of Jonah for an example of how this worked for the city of Ninevah.

There are two types of fasts. The total fast is when you do not eat or drink at all. An example of this is found in Acts 9:9. The partial fast is a restricted diet. An example of this is in Daniel 10:3.

Public and private fasting. Fasting is a personal matter between an individual and God. It is to be done in private and not boasted about (Matthew 6:16-18). Leaders, however, may also call a public fast and request the whole church to fast (Joel 2:15).

God's chosen fast. Isaiah 58 describes God's "chosen" or divinely approved fast. God's chosen fast is one:
-Where you humble yourself before God: Verse 5
-To lose the bonds of wickedness: Verse 6
-Which undoes heavy burdens: Verse 6
-That frees the oppressed: Verse 6
-Done with unselfish motives and manifested charity: Verse 7

The results of fasting. When you fast, God begins to reveal Himself to you. The Father says, *"Then you shall call, and the Lord will answer; You shall cry, and He will say, `Here am I'" (Isaiah 58:9).* Other results of fasting revealed in Isaiah 58 are:

-Illumination: Verses 8 and 10 declare that the dark periods of your life will become like noonday. When others think they have extinguished your spiritual light, it will rise again and break forth like the morning.
-Direction: Verse 11 promises that "the Lord will guide you continually."
-Provision: Verse 11 declares God will "satisfy your soul in drought." This can apply to both material and spiritually lean times. Verse 11 also describes unlimited spiritual resources. You will be like a "well watered garden," and "a spring of water whose waters do not fail."
-Rejuvenation: Verse 11 declares God will "strengthen your bones" and verse 8 proclaims that "your healing shall spring forth speedily."
-Restoration: Verse 12 indicates that you and your spiritual seed "shall build the old waste places...raise up the foundations of many generations...And you shall be called the Repairer of the Breach, The Restorer of Streets to Dwell In."

25

Prayer with fasting was practiced in the early Church and Paul encourages us to "give ourselves" to it (Acts 14:23; 1 Corinthians 7:5).

DEALING WITH FASTING:

Consider making fasting part of your spiritual discipline. Perhaps a weekly, monthly, or annual fast--or as the Lord leads you.

Length of the fast. How long you fast depend upon what God impresses on your spirit. He may lead you to fast a brief or lengthy time. Remember the story of Esau and Jacob? Jacob was originally making a meal for himself but denied himself in order to obtain the birthright. How much better if Esau had fasted that meal!

How to begin. If you have never fasted, start by fasting one meal. Next you might try fasting from sundown one day to sundown the next night, which is the measure of the Old Testament day. Then you might increase your fasting to more lengthy periods of time. You should always drink water on long fasts. You can go without food for long periods, but water is needed to maintain bodily functions.

WHAT GOD'S WORD SAYS ABOUT FASTING:

Alarmed, Jehoshaphat resolved to inquire of the Lord, and he proclaimed a fast for all Judah. (2 Chronicles 20:3)

I have not departed from the commands of his lips; I have treasured the words of his mouth more than my daily bread. (Job 23:12)

Study Isaiah 58 which reveals God's Chosen Fast.

So we fasted and petitioned our God about this, and he answered our prayer. (Ezra 8:23)

When I heard these things, I sat down and wept. For some days I mourned and fasted and prayed before the God of heaven. (Nehemiah 1:4)

So I turned to the Lord God and pleaded with him in prayer and petition, in fasting, and in sackcloth and ashes. (Daniel 9:3)

The Ninevites believed God. They declared a fast, and all of them, from the greatest to the least, put on sackcloth... When God saw what they did and how they turned from their evil ways, he had compassion and did not bring upon them the destruction he had threatened. (Jonah 3:5 and 10)

So I turned to the Lord God and pleaded with him in prayer and petition, in fasting, and in sackcloth and ashes. (Joel 1:14)

"Even now,' declares the Lord, "return to me with all your heart, with fasting and weeping and mourning. Rend your heart and not your garments. Return to the Lord your God, for he is gracious and compassionate, slow to anger and abounding in love, and he relents from sending calamity." (Joel 2:12-13)

Declare a holy fast; call a sacred assembly. Summon the elders and all who live in the land to the house of the Lord your God, and cry out to the Lord. (Joel 1:14)

Then Jesus was led by the Spirit into the desert to be tempted by the devil. After fasting forty days and forty nights, he was hungry. (Matthew 4:1-2)

When you fast, do not look somber as the hypocrites do, for they disfigure their faces to show men they are fasting. I tell you the truth, they have received their reward in full. But when you fast, put oil on your head and wash your face, so that it will not be obvious to men that you are fasting, but only to your Father, who is unseen; and your Father, who sees what is done in secret, will reward you. (Matthew 6:16-18)

While they were worshiping the Lord and fasting, the Holy Spirit said, "Set apart for me Barnabas and Saul for the work to which I have called them." So after they had fasted and prayed, they placed their hands on them and sent them off. (Acts 13:2-3)

Paul and Barnabas appointed elders for them in each church and, with prayer and fasting, committed them to the Lord, in whom they had put their trust. (Acts 14:23)

Study these Biblical examples of fasting.
-Abraham's servant fasted while seeking the right bride for Isaac (Genesis 24:33).
-Moses fasted for 40 days and nights while receiving the revelations of the law and the tabernacle (Exodus 34).
-Hannah fasted for a child (2 Samuel 1:7-8).
-Nehemiah fasted for the restoration of Jerusalem (Nehemiah 1:4).
-The Jews fasted for deliverance following Haman's evil decree of death (Esther 4).
-The entire city of Ninevah fasted in response to Jonah's call for repentance (Jonah 3:5-10).
-David fasted prior to assuming his God-given destiny as King of Israel (1 Samuel 31).
-Daniel fasted for 21 days and received the message from God that was the turning point for the Hebrews in captivity.
-Jehoshaphat proclaimed a fast prior to battle (2 Chronicles 20:3).
-Ezra called a fast of repentance for the exiles by the river Ahava (Ezra 8-9).
-Jesus fasted prior to entering His ministry (Matthew 4).
-The Apostle Paul fasted after his conversion (Acts 9).
-It was during a time of fasting that Peter received his commission to share the Gospel with the Gentiles and Cornelius was prepared to receive the revelation (Acts 10).
-The disciples were fasting and praying when the Holy Spirit separated Paul and Barnabas for missionary service (Acts 13:2).
Reasons for fasting.

-In response to a message from God: Jonah 3:5

-During times of testing: Luke 4:1
-During the threat of national calamity or war: 2 Chronicles 20:3
-When revelation was needed from God: Daniel 9:3-4
-When making decisions: Acts 13:2-3
-When making special requests before authorities: Esther 4:16
-To prepare for confrontation with demonic activity: Mark 9:29
-To humble one's self: Psalms 35:13; 69:10
-To repent of sin: Joel 2:12
-To feed the poor, both physically and spiritually: Isaiah 58:7
-To be heard of God: 2 Samuel 12:16,22; Jonah 3:5,10
-To loose bands of wickedness, lift heavy burdens,
 set the oppressed free, and break every bondage: Isaiah 58:6

CHAPTER FOUR

The "it" of Afflictions
(Healing)

DEFINITION: Healing, as used in a biblical sense, refers to being made whole and restored spiritually, emotionally, mentally, and physically. It is also called divine healing because it is when the one true God reveals His nature, fulfills His promises, and acts upon His provision in the atonement of Christ by curing a person and making him whole in body, soul, and spirit.

FACTS ABOUT HEALING:

Sickness entered the world through sin. God never intended for the spiritual sickness of sin or emotional, mental, or physical illness to be part of our world. Sickness entered the world through sin (Genesis 3). Although God sometimes uses it as punishment on sinners (Deuteronomy 28:22-35), sickness is not a sign of personal sin. See the story of the man born blind in John 9.

Reasons for sickness. Although sickness entered the world through sin, not all sickness is caused by personal sin. Spiritual sickness is, of course, caused by sin and it is true that sometimes physical conditions result from sin. But sickness can also result from a violation of natural laws, i.e., improper diet, overworking, lack of exercise, abuse of drugs and alcohol, or even violating the natural law of gravity. Satanic attacks also result in sickness as in the case of Job (Job chapter 2). Some sickness is caused by demons. See the accounts in Matthew 12:22-23; Matthew 9:32-33; Mark 9:25; and Luke 13:11.

God views sickness as captivity (Job 42:10); bondage (Luke 13:16); and oppression (Acts 10:38).

Healing is a gift from God. The psalmist declared: *"Praise the Lord, O my soul; all my inmost being, praise his holy name. Praise the Lord, O my soul, and forget not all his benefits--who forgives all your sins and heals all your diseases" (Psalms 103:1-3).*

All true healing comes from God, even when the gifts of natural or medical means are used.

Spiritual healing--salvation from sin--is the greatest healing. It addresses sinful behaviors that need to be corrected. Spiritual "sickness" is anything that adversely affects your spirit.

Emotional healing is the healing of damaged emotions. No wound is so deep that God cannot heal it. A wounded spirit is difficult to bear (Proverbs 18:13). This is why you need inner healing. Your spirit becomes wounded by sin (Psalm 38:4-6,8); by your enemies (Psalm143:3-4,7); and through anger, bitterness, and unforgiveness. These attitudes must be dealt with in order to receive emotional healing.

Mental healing is a healing of your mind from hurts, actual brain damage, or wrong thinking.

God has redeemed you from the curse of sin. This includes the curse of sickness that resulted from sin (Galatians 3:13). This does not mean you will never be sick, but it does mean that healing is available for every condition.

Healing is a benefit of the death of Jesus on the cross. The prophet Isaiah declared: *"But he was pierced for our transgressions, he was crushed for our iniquities; the punishment that brought us peace was upon him, and by his wounds we are healed" (Isaiah 53:5).*

Some believe that divine healings no longer occur, but the Bible says Jesus is the same yesterday, today, and forever (Hebrews 13:8). As Jesus healed in Bible times, so He heals today. There are also many medically documented healings that have occurred after prayer to God.

Doctors and legitimate medicines are not in opposition to the Bible. Every good gift--such as doctors, legitimate medicines, and natural remedies--come from God   (James 1:17). There is no conflict between divine healing and medical healing.   Even when doctors and medications are used to facilitate healing, the ultimate healing is from God.

God heals all sickness and diseases--event those classified as incurable or terminal by medicine, because nothing is impossible to God (Luke 1:37).

All believers can minister healing. Jesus declared: *"And these signs shall follow them that believe; In my name shall they cast out devils; they shall speak with new tongues; They shall take up serpents; and if they drink any deadly thing, it shall not hurt them; they shall lay hands on the sick, and they shall recover" (Mark 16:17-18).*

Some believers have a special gift of healing. First Corinthians 12:9 speaks of those who have a special gift of ministering healing.

There is a sickness unto death; John 11:4 speaks of a sickness that was not unto death. Second Kings 13:14 speaks of a time when Elisha was sick of the illness of which he would die. As a believer, you should continue to pray for healing unless God reveals that it is a person's time to die. Sometimes a person will say, "I am ready and believe it is my time to go be with the Lord." If they have that assurance, then you need to help them prepare by setting things in order and being with them in death. Draw encouragement from 1 Corinthians 15:51-55; Psalm 116:15; 2 Corinthians 5:1-8.

Not everyone is healed immediately. Job was healed when he forgave his friends and prayed for them. Unforgiveness can block healing, as can personal sin. Sometimes a person does not receive healing because they don't believe in divine healing. Some people don't really want healing because they are using their illness as an excuse not to work or to draw government assistance. Jesus delayed ministering to Lazarus because He had a greater miracle planned. There are many variables involved in healing, and we cannot accurately judge why healing does not occur immediately. This is one of the secret things that belongs to the Lord (Deuteronomy 29:29). Not everyone who hears the gospel gets saved. Not everyone to whom healing is ministered receives healing.

The end result of sickness for a believer is that it is either for the glory of God through divine healing (John 9:3) or it is a sickness unto death to usher you into Christ's presence (2 Kings 13:14). As a believer, you will be either healed in time or eternity, but you will be healed.

DEALING WITH HEALING:

Determine the healing needed. Is its spiritual, emotional, mental, or physical or a combination of these? In order to be whole, each of these areas must be healed. For example, a person may ask for healing for a vision problem, but he may not know Jesus as Savior and his greater need is for spiritual healing.

Study what God's Word says about healing. This will increase your faith to receive and minister healing.

Eliminate any preconceived notions concerning healing. Doctrines such as "healing is not for today" must be eliminated in order to believe for healing. Just as one believes and confesses the Lord Jesus in order to be saved, one must believe and confess He heals in order to be healed.

Seek first the greatest miracle of spiritual healing. Healing from sin is vital to healing in the mental, emotional, and physical realms. If you do not know Christ as your Savior, you need a spiritual healing.

Determine if any conditions are caused by errant behavior. For example, smoking, drugs, and alcohol addictions can affect a person physically, emotionally, and mentally. The behaviors contributing to conditions in any area must be bound spiritual and revoked lest *"a worse thing come upon you" (John 5:14).*

Pray for healing. If the condition is caused by demons, pray for deliverance. If you need an emotional healing, confess your feelings to God and ask Him to heal your inner wounds. Bind Satanic influences over your mind if you need a mental deliverance. Pray for physical healing if you are sick.   If you are in a Bible believing church, call for the elders to anoint and pray over you: *"Is any of you sick? He should call the elders of the church to pray over him and anoint him with oil in the name of the Lord. And the prayer offered in faith will make the sick person well; the Lord will raise him up" (James 5:14-15).*

Receive your healing by faith. Just as you received salvation by faith--with no immediate visible signs apparent--so you can receive healing by faith even if there are no immediate signs are apparent. Sometimes there are miraculous signs accompanying a healing. At other times, the healing occurs gradually. When you receive salvation, the outward changes in your life are apparent gradually, and the same is sometimes true in healing.

Act upon your healing. James 2:17 says that faith without action is dead. Do something you could not do before prayer. For example, if you could not bend over, bend over. If you have been under a doctor's care, return to your doctor to confirm your healing.

Maintain your healing. Stand in faith on the Word of God. Rather than believing your symptoms, believe God's Word. Continue to stand on the promises of healing in God's Word. Commit yourself to total trust in God for healing. Change your lifestyle, if your former way of life contributed to your sickness. Resist the attempts by Satan to cause sickness to return.

Do not become discouraged if healing is not received immediately. Some healings in the Bible were instantaneous, others were delayed. Continue to pray for healing. Continue to build your faith in the Word of God. Where applicable, change your lifestyle and eliminate sinful and unhealthy practices. Claim the promises of God for healing.

WHAT GOD'S WORD SAYS ABOUT HEALING:

Old Testament

Genesis 17:18-19: God promised to heal Sara's barrenness.
Genesis 21:1-7: Sara's barrenness is healed.
Genesis 20:17: God healed Abimelech.
Exodus 4:1-18: Moses' leprous hand.
Exodus 15:25-26: God reveals His name as "Jehovah-Rapha" which means, "The Lord Your Physician." He promised that none of the diseases of Egypt would come upon Israel.
Exodus 23:25: God promised to take away sickness from among His people.
Leviticus 13:1-46; 14:1-32: Regulations regarding leprosy.
Leviticus 15:1-33: Health regulations.
Leviticus 16:29-30: Healing of sins.
Numbers 12:1-15: Leprosy of Miriam and Aaron.
Numbers 16:41-50: A plague affects Israel.
Numbers 21:4-9: Healing through the symbolic serpent of brass.
Deuteronomy 7:15: Obedience to God results in health.
Deuteronomy 28:1-68: Sickness results when you do not observe God's law.
Deuteronomy 29:22: The Lord lays sickness on the land.
Deuteronomy 30:20: God is life and length of days.
Deuteronomy 32:39: God wounds and heals.
Deuteronomy 7:15; 28:60: Diseases of Egypt.
Judges 13:2-24: Manoah's wife is healed by a "man of God."
1 Samuel 6:3: A trespass offering brought healing.
1 Samuel 16:14-23: An evil spirit troubles Saul.
1 Kings 5:23; 2 Chronicles 16:12: Diseases in the feet.
1 Kings 8:37-40: Plagues in the land.
1 Kings 13:4-6: A man with a withered hand.
1 Kings 17:17-24: Elijah raises a child from the dead.
2 Kings 1:2; 8:8-9: Shall I recover of this disease?
2 Kings 2:19-22: Healing of waters by Elisha.
2 Kings 4:8-37: Raising of the Shunamite's son.
2 Kings 5:1-14: The healing of Naaman.
2 Kings 13:14,21: Elisha is sick with a sickness unto death.
2 Kings 20:1-11: Hezekiah's illness.

2 Chronicles 6:26-31: Prayer of repentance and sickness.
2 Chronicles 7:14: "I will heal their land."
2 Chronicles 16:12: A man with a serious disease does not seek God.
2 Chronicles 20:9: God hears when you cry in affliction.
2 Chronicles 21:12-30: An incurable disease of the bowels.
2 Chronicles 24:25: Disease is called great.
2 Chronicles 26:19: Uzziah's leprosy.
2 Chronicles 30:20: Healing of people by Hezekiah's prayers.
2 Chronicles 32:24-26: Hezekiah's illness.
Job 1-2: These chapters reveal the sources of Job's problems, including his sickness.
Job 5:18; 30:18: Job talks about His disease.
Psalms 6:2-3: "O Lord heal me."
Psalms 27:1: "The Lord is the strength of my life."
Psalms 30:2: "I cried and you healed me."
Psalms 32:3-5: Acknowledged sin results in healing.
Psalms 34:19-20: "Many are the afflictions of the righteous, but the Lord delivers him out of them all."
Psalms 38:3,7: Anger and sin affects your health; disease is called "loathsome."
Psalms 41:1-8: "Heal my soul for I have sinned against thee." Disease is called evil.
Psalms 42:11; 43:5: God is the health of your countenance.
Psalms 42:1-5: Healing for a downcast spirit.
Psalms 55:1-2: Persevering prayer and healing.
Psalms 67:2: "That Your way may be known upon earth, Your saving healing among all nations."
Psalms 72:13: You are to pity the weak.
Psalms 91:9,10: "Neither shall any plague come nigh your dwelling."
Psalms 103:1-5: "Forget not His benefits...Who heals all your diseases."
Psalms 105:37: Israel came forth without one feeble person among them. Three million people were all well and strong.
Psalms 107:17-20: "He sent His Word and healed them."
Psalms 119:25-28: You are strengthened by the Word.
Psalms 119:67: "Before I was afflicted, I went astray."
Psalms 147:3: "Who heals all your diseases." Healing for a broken heart.
Psalms 105:37: "He brought them forth...not one feeble among them."
Proverbs 3:7-8: How to be healthy.
Proverbs 4:20-23: The issues of life are affected by your heart attitude. God's promises are life to those that find them and health to all their flesh.
Proverbs 12:18: The tongue of the wise brings healing.
Proverbs 15:4,30: A wholesome tongue is life; good reports affect health.
Proverbs 16:24: The Word of God brings healing to the bones.
Proverbs 17:22: A broken spirit affects the bones.
Ecclesiastes 3:3: There is a time to heal.
Ecclesiastes 5:17: Sorrow and wrath are related to sickness.
Isaiah 6:10: Understanding, conversion, healing.
Isaiah 19:22: When God is entreated He heals.
Isaiah 32:3-4: Healing is part of the Kingdom of God.

Isaiah 33:24: Inhabitants shall say, "I am not sick."
Isaiah 35:5-6: Healing in the Millennium.
Isaiah 38:1-12,16: Hezekiah's illness and his return to health.
Isaiah 53:5: We are promised healing and deliverance through the atonement.
Isaiah 57:18-19: Draw near for healing.
Isaiah 58:8: Health shall spring forth.
Isaiah 61:1: Jesus was sent to bind up the brokenhearted (emotional healing).
Isaiah 58:8: Health springing forth speedily.
Jeremiah 3:22: God heals backsliding when you return to Him.
Jeremiah 8:14-15; 20-22: A time of healing. Bitterness of sin is tied to physical health.
Jeremiah 15:18: How to deal with an incurable wound.
Jeremiah 14:19: Is there no healing for us?
Jeremiah 17:14: "Heal me and I will be healed."
Jeremiah 30:12-17: God will restore health.
Jeremiah 33:6: "I will cure them."
Jeremiah 51:8-9: Healing of Babylon.
Lamentations 2:13: "Who can heal you?"
Lamentations 3:33: "God does not willingly afflict."
Ezekiel 14:19: "Is there no healing for us?"
Ezekiel 17:14: "Heal me and I will be healed."
Ezekiel 30:17: "I will restore health."
Ezekiel 30:12-13: Incurable wounds medicine cannot heal.
Ezekiel 30:21: What God breaks cannot be healed.
Ezekiel 33:6: "I will heal them."
Ezekiel 34:4,16,21: A warning to shepherds who have not healed.
Ezekiel 47:8-12: Healing of the waters.
Daniel 4:34,36: Nebuchadnezzar's healing.
Hosea 5:13: Man cannot cure a wound inflicted by God.
Hosea 6:1: "He has torn and He will heal."
Hosea 7:1: Healing for Israel.
Hosea 11:3: "They knew not I healed them."
Hosea 14:4: "I will heal their backslidings."
Nahum 3:19: A terminal condition.
Zechariah 11:16: A warning to shepherds who do not heal.
Malachi 4:2: Healing in His wings.

New Testament

Matthew 8:13: The point of contact sets the time.
Matthew 8:17: Jesus bore our sicknesses.
Matthew 10:1: Power over sickness and demons is given to the disciples.
Matthew 18:19-21: Any two agreeing receive what is asked.
Mark 2:17: Christ came to heal sinners.
Mark 3:15-17: Christ gives power to heal sicknesses.
Mark 4:18-19: Healing is part of the anointing; Jesus was sent to heal.

Mark 11:24: If you believe when you pray (not after you receive), you will receive.
Mark 16:18: In Jesus' name believers will heal sick and cast out demons.
Luke 5:31: The sick need a physician.
Luke 7:6: Unworthiness is viewed by Jesus as faith.
Luke 7:22-23: The most convincing argument is experience.
Luke 17:6: Small faith can bring great results.
Luke 18:7-8: Do not give up before your answer comes.
John 6:53-58: The body and blood of Jesus bring life.
John 10:10: Jesus came so that you can have life. Satan came to kill, steal, and destroy.
John 11:1-45: A sickness not healed immediately leads to a greater miracle.
John 14:12-13: The works Jesus did, you are to do.
John 15:7: The importance of abiding in Christ in relation to asking and receiving.
John 16:24: Ask in His name and you will receive.
Romans 2:4 The goodness of God leads to repentance.
2 Corinthians 4:16: Your outward man perishes, but your inward man can be renewed.
Ephesians 3:20-21: God has the power to work in you above all that you ask or think.
Philippians 2:25-27: The illness of Epaphroditus.
Colossians 4:14: Luke, a physician, was part of Paul's evangelistic team.
2 Timothy 4:20: Trophimus' illness.
Hebrews 4:15: He is touched with your infirmities.
Hebrews 11:1: Faith is the evidence of things (healing) not seen.
James 1:8: You must ask in faith and not waver.
James 1:17: Every good gift (healing, doctors, legitimate medicine) is from God.
James 5:14-15: Call the elders for anointing with oil, the prayer of faith, healing, and
forgiveness.
1 Peter 2:24: You are healed by His wounds.
1 John 3:22: Whatever you ask you can receive if you are obedient.
3 John 1:2: Health is related to the condition of your soul.
Mark 7:36, 8:26; Matthew 8:4: Do not sensationalize healing.
Revelation 20:2-3: When Satan is bound, there is no more sickness and death.
Revelation 21:4: The final healing: No more sickness and death.

CHAPTER FIFTH

The "it" of Lack of Faith

DEFINITION: Faith is belief or trust in someone or something without overt proof. Biblically, faith is being sure of what we hope for and certain of what we do not see (Hebrews 11:1). The basic tenets of our faith are based on the Gospel of the Lord Jesus Christ.

FACTS ABOUT FAITH:

Faith is not the same as "mind over matter." Mind over matter teaches that man can overcome all problems by using his mind, reason, or willpower. These teachings are man-centered. They rely on self and not on God. "Mind over matter" is not based on the Word of God. Faith is God-centered, not man-centered. It is a gift of God, not something you produce through your mental abilities.

Faith can be misplaced. Faith is not just "faith in general"--it is directed faith in the one and true God. You can have misdirected faith in natural resources (Psalm 44:6; 20:7); great men (Psalm 146:3); idols (Isaiah 42:17); false prophets (Jeremiah 7:4,8); wealth (Psalm 52:7); friends (Psalm 41:9); and by placing trust in yourself instead of God (Proverbs 28:26).

You are commanded to have faith in God. Jesus commanded: *"Have faith in God" (Mark 11:22).*

It is impossible to please God without faith. You must not only believe in God, but you must believe that He acts in your behalf: *"And without faith it is impossible to please God, because anyone who comes to him must believe that he exists and that he rewards those who earnestly seek him" (Hebrews 11:6).*

Atheism is an extreme form of lack of faith. It is refusing to believe that God exists (Psalm 14:1).

Saving faith is a gift of God. God grants everyone a measure of faith in order for them to obtain salvation: *"But what does it say? 'The word is near you; it is in your mouth and in your heart,' that is, the word of faith we are proclaiming: That if you confess with your mouth, 'Jesus is Lord,' and believe in your heart that God raised him from the dead, you will be saved. For it is with your heart that you believe and are justified, and it is with your mouth that you confess and are saved" (Romans 10:8-10).* It is through faith you are saved: *"For it is by grace you have been saved, through faith--and this not from yourselves, it is the gift of God--not by works, so that no one can boast" (Ephesians 2:8-10).*

Faith cannot be increased by works. You cannot increase your faith by doing things for God. Faith, however, is demonstrated through your works (James 2:14-18).

Faith increases through the Word of God. The Bible reveals that everyone is given a certain amount of faith as a gift from God (Romans 12:3b). Your faith can be increased by studying the

Word of God because the scriptures were recorded to increase your faith (John 20:31). The Apostle Paul declared: *"Consequently, faith comes from hearing the message, and the message is heard through the word of Christ"* (Romans 10:17).

Faith affects how God works in your life. There are various levels of faith that can be developed after your conversion to Christ. Jesus spoke of people who did not use their faith as being "faithless" (Matthew 17:17). He spoke of those with little faith (Matthew 6:30; 8:26; 14:31; Luke 12:28) and of those with great faith (Matthew 8:10; 15:28; Luke 7:9). Jesus did no great works in Nazareth because of their lack of faith (Matthew 13:58). When a centurion came to Him with a request, Jesus said: *"Go! It will be done just as you believed it would." (Matthew 8:13)* and to a woman seeking healing *"...your faith has healed you" (Matthew 9:22)*.

Faith is an important spiritual virtue. Faith is a shield against Satanic attacks (Ephesians 6:16). Faith is the victory that helps you resist the enemy (1 Peter 5:9) and overcome the world (1 John 5:4). Faith gives you endurance (James 1:3) and results in blessings in your life (1 Peter 1:5). Faith gives assurance of eternal life (John 5:24) and dispels the darkness of this world (John 12:46). You are sanctified by faith (Galatians 2:20) and receive the promise of the Holy Spirit by faith (Galatians 3:14). Faith is a fruit of the Holy Spirit that is to be manifested in your life (Galatians5:22-23). Christ dwells in your heart by faith (Ephesians 3:17). Your entire Christian walk is based on faith (Romans 1:17; 2 Corinthians 5:7).

DEALING WITH FAITH:

Confess your lack of faith as sin. *"...for what is not of faith is sin"* (Romans 14:23). Lack of faith means you do not believe God at His Word. As the father who brought his ailing child to Jesus, cry out by faith, *"Lord I believe. Help me overcome my unbelief!" (Mark 9:24)*.

Immerse yourself in the Word of God. Faith is increased through hearing, reading, and studying God's Word (Romans 10:17). There are approximately 500 references to faith and belief in the New Testament. Read through the New Testament and study each reference to faith and belief.

Spend time in prayer. Prayer is linked with faith in Matthew 17:20 and James 5:15. As you pray regularly and receive answers to your prayers, your faith will increase.

WHAT GOD'S WORD SAYS ABOUT FAITH:

The fool says in his heart, "There is no God." (Psalm 14:1)

Trust in the Lord with all your heart and lean not on your own understanding; in all your ways acknowledge him, and he will make your paths straight.   (Proverbs 3:5-6)

Then Jesus said to the centurion, "Go! It will be done just as you believed it would." (Matthew 8:13)

"...your faith has healed you" (Matthew 9:22)

"According to your faith will it be done to you..." (Matthew 9:29)

Now He did not do many mighty works there because of their unbelief. (Matthews 13:58)

Then the disciples came to Jesus privately and said, "Why could we not cast it out?" So Jesus said to them, "Because of your unbelief; for assuredly, I say to you, if you have faith as a mustard seed, you will say to this mountain, 'Move from here to there,' and it will move; and nothing will be impossible for you. (Matthew 17:19-21, NKJV)

If you believe, you will receive whatever you ask for in prayer."   (Matthew 21:22)

He said to his disciples, "Why are you so afraid? Do you still have no faith?" (Mark 4:40)

He said to her, "Daughter, your faith has healed you. Go in peace and be freed from your suffering." (Mark 5:34)

Ignoring what they said, Jesus told the synagogue ruler, "Don't be afraid; just believe." (Mark 5:36)

"Lord I believe. Help me overcome my unbelief!" (Mark 9:24).

"Go," said Jesus, "your faith has healed you." Immediately he received his sight and followed Jesus along the road. (Mark 10:52)

"Have faith in God," Jesus answered. "I tell you the truth, if anyone says to this mountain, 'Go, throw yourself into the sea,' and does not doubt in his heart but believes that what he says will happen, it will be done for him. Therefore, I tell you, whatever you ask for in prayer, believe that you have received it, and it will be yours." (Mark 11:22-24)

Later He appeared to the eleven as they sat at the table; and He rebuked their unbelief and hardness of heart, because they did not believe those who had seen Him after He had risen. (Mark 15:14, NKJV)

Whoever believes and is baptized will be saved, but whoever does not believe will be condemned. (Mark 16:16)

For nothing is impossible with God. (Luke 1:37)

"Where is your faith?" he asked his disciples. (Luke 8:22)

"Consider how the lilies grow. They do not labor or spin. Yet I tell you, not even Solomon in all his splendor was dressed like one of these. If that is how God clothes the grass of the field, which is here today, and tomorrow is thrown into the fire, how much more will he clothe you, O you of little faith! And do not set your heart on what you will eat or drink; do not worry about it.

For the pagan world runs after all such things, and your Father knows that you need them. But seek his kingdom, and these things will be given to you as well." (Luke 12:27-31)

If they do not listen to Moses and the Prophets, they will not be convinced even if someone rises from the dead. (Luke 16:31)

The apostles said to the Lord, "Increase our faith!" (Luke 17:5)

Then he said to him, "Rise and go; your faith has made you well." (Luke 17:19)

Jesus said to him, "Receive your sight; your faith has healed you." Immediately he received his sight and followed Jesus, praising God. When all the people saw it, they also praised God. (Luke 18:42-43)

If you are the Christ," they said, "tell us." Jesus answered, If I tell you, you will not believe me, and if I asked you, you would not answer. (Luke 22:67-68)

The apostles said to the Lord, "Increase our faith!" (Luke 27:5)

Yet to all who received him, to those who believed in his name, he gave the right to become children of God--children born not of natural descent, nor of human decision or a husband's will, but born of God. (John 1:12-13)

For God so loved the world that he gave his one and only Son, that whoever believes in him shall not perish but have eternal life. For God did not send his Son into the world to condemn the world, but to save the world through him. Whoever believes in him is not condemned, but whoever does not believe stands condemned already because he has not believed in the name of God's one and only Son. (John 3:16-18)

Whoever believes in the Son has eternal life, but whoever rejects the Son will not see life, for God's wrath remains on him. (John 3:36)

Unless you people see miraculous signs and wonders, Jesus told him, you will never believe. (John 4:48)

"I tell you the truth, whoever hears my word and believes him who sent me has eternal life and will not be condemned; he has crossed over from death to life." (John 5:24)

I tell you the truth, he who believes has everlasting life. (John 6:47)

The words I have spoken to you are spirit and they are life. Yet there are some of you who do not believe. (John 6:63)

For even his own brothers did not believe in him. (John 7:5)

I told you that you would die in your sins; if you do not believe that I am [the one I claim to be], you will indeed die in your sins. (John 8:24)

Even after Jesus had done all these miraculous signs in their presence, they still would not believe in him. (John 12:37)

I am come a light into the world, that whosoever believeth on me should not abide in darkness. (John 12:46)

But these are written that you may believe that Jesus is the Christ, the Son of God, and that by believing you may have life in his name. (John 20:31)

By faith in the name of Jesus, this man whom you see and know was made strong. It is Jesus' name and the faith that comes through him that has given this complete healing to him, as you can all see. (Acts 3:16)

I am sending you to them to open their eyes and turn them from darkness to light, and from the power of Satan to God, so that they may receive forgiveness of sins and a place among those who are sanctified by faith in me. (Acts 26:17-18)

For in the gospel a righteousness from God is revealed, a righteousness that is by faith from first to last, just as it is written: "The righteous will live by faith." (Romans 1:17)

Read Romans chapters 3-4 for several key references to faith.

Yet he (Abraham) did not waver through unbelief regarding the promise of God, but was strengthened in his faith and gave glory to God, being fully persuaded that God had power to do what he had promised. (Romans 4:20-21)

Therefore, since we have been justified through faith, we have peace with God through our Lord Jesus Christ, through whom we have gained access by faith into this grace in which we now stand. And we rejoice in the hope of the glory of God. (Romans 5:1-2)

But what does it say? "The word is near you; it is in your mouth and in your heart," that is, the word of faith we are proclaiming: That if you confess with your mouth, "Jesus is Lord," and believe in your heart that God raised him from the dead, you will be saved. For it is with your heart that you believe and are justified, and it is with your mouth that you confess and are saved" (Romans 10:8-10).

Consequently, faith comes from hearing the message, and the message is heard through the word of Christ. (Romans 10:17)

My message and my preaching were not with wise and persuasive words, but with a demonstration of the Spirit's power, 5 so that your faith might not rest on men's wisdom, but on God's power. (1 Corinthians 2:4-5)

Read 1 Corinthians chapter 13. Faith is one of the three main virtues of the Christian life.

...for by faith you stand. (2 Corinthians 1:24)

Know that a man is not justified by observing the law, but by faith in Jesus Christ. So we, too, have put our faith in Christ Jesus that we may be justified by faith in Christ and not by observing the law, because by observing the law no one will be justified. (Galatians 2:16)

I have been crucified with Christ and I no longer live, but Christ lives in me. The life I live in the body, I live by faith in the Son of God, who loved me and gave himself for me. (Galatians 2:20)

Clearly no one is justified before God by the law, because, "The righteous will live by faith." (Galatians 3:11)

(Read Galatians chapter 3 for several key references to faith)

For it is by grace you have been saved, through faith--and this not from yourselves, it is the gift of God--not by works, so that no one can boast. (Ephesians 2:8-10)

In addition to all this, take up the shield of faith, with which you can extinguish all the flaming arrows of the evil one. (Ephesians 6:16)

If you point these things out to the brothers, you will be a good minister of Christ Jesus, brought up in the truths of the faith and of the good teaching that you have followed. (1 Timothy 4:6)

Don't let anyone look down on you because you are young, but set an example for the believers in speech, in life, in love, in faith and in purity. (1 Timothy 4:12)

But you, O man of God, flee these things and pursue righteousness, godliness, faith, love, patience, gentleness. Fight the good fight of faith, lay hold on eternal life, to which you were also called and have confessed the good confession in the presence of many witnesses. (1 Timothy 6:11-12)

I have fought the good fight, I have finished the race, I have kept the faith. (2 Timothy 4:7)

See to it, brothers, that none of you has a sinful, unbelieving heart that turns away from the living God. But encourage one another daily, as long as it is called Today, so that none of you may be hardened by sin's deceitfulness. (Hebrews 3:12-13)

Let us hold unswervingly to the hope we profess, for he who promised is faithful. (Hebrews 10:23)

Now faith is the assurance, the confirmation, the title deed of the things we hope for, being the proof of things we do not see, and the conviction of their reality. Faith is perceiving as real what is not revealed to the senses. (Hebrews 11:1, AMP)

And without faith it is impossible to please God, because anyone who comes to him must believe that he exists and that he rewards those who earnestly seek him. (Hebrews 11:6)

(Study Hebrews 11 in its entirety. It defines faith and gives multiple examples of faith in action.)

If any of you lacks wisdom, he should ask God, who gives generously to all without finding fault, and it will be given to him. But when he asks, he must believe and not doubt, because he who doubts is like a wave of the sea, blown and tossed by the wind. That man should not think he will receive anything from the Lord;   he is a double-minded man, unstable in all he does. (James 1:5-8)

Study James chapter 2 for numerous references to faith.

And the prayer offered in faith will make the sick person well; the Lord will raise him up. If he has sinned, he will be forgiven. (James 5:15)

Praise be to the God and Father of our Lord Jesus Christ! In his great mercy he has given us new birth into a living hope through the resurrection of Jesus Christ from the dead, 4 and into an inheritance that can never perish, spoil or fade--kept in heaven for you, who through faith are shielded by God's power until the coming of the salvation that is ready to be revealed in the last time. (1 Peter 1:3-5)

In this you greatly rejoice, though now for a little while you may have had to suffer grief in all kinds of trials. These have come so that your faith--of greater worth than gold, which perishes even though refined by fire--may be proved genuine and may result in praise, glory and honor when Jesus Christ is revealed. Though you have not seen him, you love him; and even though you do not see him now, you believe in him and are filled with an inexpressible and glorious joy, for you are receiving the goal of your faith, the salvation of your souls. (1 Peter 1:6-,9)

And this is his command: to believe in the name of his Son, Jesus Christ, and to love one another as he commanded us. (1 John 3:23)

...for everyone born of God overcomes the world. This is the victory that has overcome the world, even our faith. (1 John 5:4)

Dear friends, although I was very eager to write to you about the salvation we share, I felt I had to write and urge you to contend for the faith that was once for all entrusted to the saints. (Jude 3)

But you, dear friends, build yourselves up in your most holy faith and pray in the Holy Spirit (Jude 20)

But the cowardly, the unbelieving, the vile, the murderers, the sexually immoral, those who practice magic arts, the idolaters and all liars--their place will be in the fiery lake of burning sulfur. This is the second death."   (Revelation 21:8)

CHAPTER SIX

The "it" of Lack of Gift of the Holy Spirit

DEFINITION: The word "spiritual" means "characterized or controlled by the Holy Spirit." A "gift" is something freely given from one person to another. A spiritual gift is a supernatural ability given by the Holy Spirit to a believer for the purpose of service in the Body of Christ.

FACTS ABOUT GIFTS OF THE HOLY SPIRIT:

There is a difference between the "gift" and "gifts" of the Holy Spirit. The "gift" was given at Pentecost (Acts 2) when the Holy Spirit was given in answer to the promise of Jesus: *"And I will pray the Father, and He shall give you another Comforter...Even the Spirit of truth..."(John 14:16-17a).* "Gifts" are supernatural abilities given by the Holy Spirit to enable effective ministry, and are distributed to each believer as the Holy Spirit wills.

There is a difference between spiritual gifts and natural talents. A talent is a natural ability inherited at birth or developed through training. A spiritual gift is a supernatural ability given by the Holy Spirit to be used for specific spiritual purposes.

The purposes of the gifts of the Holy Spirit are listed in Ephesians 4:12-15. The purposes are to perfect the saints, promote the work of the ministry, and edify Christ and the Church. The goals of these spiritual gifts are that we will become united in the faith, develop our knowledge of Christ, develop in perfection, with Christ as our model, become stable, not be deceived by false doctrines, and mature spiritually in Christ.

There are many gifts which come from one source. The source of spiritual gifts is the Holy Spirit who gives and operates these gifts in the lives of believers (1 Corinthians 12:4-7).

Each believer has at least one spiritual gift. *"Each one should use whatever gift he has received to serve others, faithfully administering God's grace in its various forms" (1 Peter 4:10).* See also 1 Corinthians 12:7, 11.

You are only a steward of your spiritual gifts. A steward does not own that with which he works. He uses something given to him in behalf of the person who gave it to him. You are a steward of your spiritual gifts to be used for the advancement of the Gospel (1 Corinthians 4:1).

The key to using spirit gifts is love. See 1 Corinthians chapter 13.

A spiritual gift can be abused. You abuse spiritual gifts by not using the gifts given to you (1 Timothy 4:14, 2 Timothy 1:6); attempting to use gifts not given to you (Acts 8:20-21; 19:15-16); and not using gifts properly (1 Corinthians 14:33,40).

The main passages identifying spiritual gifts are Romans 12:1-8; 1 Corinthians 12:1-31; Ephesians 4:1-16; and 1 Peter 4:7-11.

Spiritual gifts include the following.

-Leadership gifts.

Apostle. An apostle is one who has a special ability to develop new churches in different places and cultures and to oversee a number of churches as a supervisor. Apostle means "a delegate, one sent with full power and authority to act for another."

Prophet. Prophecy is the ability to receive and communicate an immediate message from God to His people through a divinely-anointed utterance. A prophet is one who is in a leadership position in addition to his gift of prophesying.

Evangelist. An evangelist has a special ability to share the Gospel with non-believers in a way that men and women respond and become responsible members of the Body of Christ.

Pastor. Pastors are leaders who assume long-term responsibility for the spiritual welfare of a group of believers.

Teachers are believers who have the ability to communicate the Word of God effectively in such a way that others learn and apply what is taught. As a leadership gift, they also assume a leadership role in addition to teaching.

-Speaking gifts.

Prophecy is speaking by the special inspiration of God to communicate an immediate message to His people.

Teaching communicates the Word of God in a way that others can learn and apply what is taught.

Exhortation is the ability to draw close to individuals in time of need, counseling them correctly with the Word of God. To "exhort" means to call a person aside, to advise, recommend, admonish, encourage, or comfort.

Word of knowledge is the ability to understand things which others cannot comprehend and to share this knowledge with them under the inspiration of the Spirit.

Word of wisdom is the ability to receive insight as to how knowledge may be applied to specific needs.

-Serving gifts.

Discerning of spirits is the ability to evaluate people, doctrines, and situations as to whether they are of God or of Satan.

Leadership is the ability to make plans in accord with God's purpose and to communicate these goals to others. A person with this gift motivates others to accomplish these goals for the glory of God.

Administration. A person with the gift of administration has the ability to give direction, organize, and make decisions on behalf of others.

Faith is a special ability to believe with supernatural confidence and trust God in difficult circumstances.

Giving. A person with the gift of giving has a special ability to give material goods and financial resources to the work of the Lord. The gift of giving also includes giving time, strength, and talents to the work of the Lord. All Christians are to give to the work of the Lord, but the gift of giving is a special ability given to give above and beyond the average believer.

Helps. A person with the gift of helps assists others in their work for the Lord.

Serving is an ability to assume routine but necessary duties to free others to fulfill their giftedness.

Mercy is the ability to show special compassion on those suffering and help them

Hospitality is a special ability to provide food, lodging, and care for those in need.

-Sign gifts.

Miracles. Through a person with the gift of miracles God performs powerful acts which are beyond the possibility of occurring naturally.

Healing. A believer with the gifts of healing has the ability to let God's power flow through him to restore health apart from the use of natural methods. All believers can pray for the sick, but a believer with a healing gift is used specifically and consistently by God in this area of ministry.

Tongues is the ability to receive and communicate a message of God to His people through a language unknown to listeners, a message which is subsequently interpreted by someone with the gift of interpretation.

Interpretation of tongues is the ability to make known in a language understood by listeners a message from God given through one with the gifts of tongues.

DEALING WITH GIFTS OF THE HOLY SPIRIT:

Become a believer. You must be a believer in order to receive a spiritual gift. If you do not know Jesus Christ as Savior, confess your sins, repent, and accept Him into your life.

Receive the baptism of the Holy Spirit. See "Baptisms" in this database for guidelines to receive the baptism of the Holy Spirit.

Pray for spiritual gifts. The Apostle Paul said to desire spiritual gifts (1 Corinthians 12:31). Ask the Holy Spirit to manifest in your life the gifts necessary for you to minister effectively in the realm of your spiritual calling.

Have church elders lay hands on you to bestow and confirm your gifts. They did this for Timothy, a young minister in New Testament times (2 Timothy 1:6).

Use your spiritual gifts. God has given you spiritual gifts and expects you to use what you have been given. Read the parable of the talents in Matthew 25:14-30.

WHAT GOD'S WORD SAYS ABOUT GIFTS OF THE HOLY SPIRIT:

I long to see you so that I may impart to you some spiritual gift to make you strong--that is, that you and I may be mutually encouraged by each other's faith. (Romans 1:11-12)

Therefore, I urge you, brothers, in view of God's mercy, to offer your bodies as living sacrifices, holy and pleasing to God--this is your spiritual act of worship. Do not conform any longer to the pattern of this world, but be transformed by the renewing of your mind. Then you will be able to test and approve what God's will is his good, pleasing and perfect will. For by the grace given me I say to every one of you: Do not think of yourself more highly than you ought, but rather think of yourself with sober judgment, in accordance with the measure of faith God has given you. Just as each of us has one body with many members, and these members do not all have the same function, so in Christ we who are many form one body, and each member belongs to all the others. We have different gifts, according to the grace given us. If a man's gift is prophesying, let him use it in proportion to his faith. If it is serving, let him serve; if it is teaching, let him teach; if it is encouraging, let him encourage; if it is contributing to the needs of others, let him give generously; if it is leadership, let him govern diligently; if it is showing mercy, let him do it cheerfully. (Romans 12:1-8)

Therefore, you do not lack any spiritual gift as you eagerly wait for our Lord Jesus Christ to be revealed. He will keep you strong to the end, so that you will be blameless on the day of our Lord Jesus Christ. God, who has called you into fellowship with his Son Jesus Christ our Lord, is faithful. (1 Corinthians 1:7-9)

Read- 1 Corinthians chapter 12.

Read- 1 Corinthians chapter 14.

But to each one of us grace has been given as Christ apportioned it. This is why it says: "When he ascended on high, he led captives in his train and gave gifts to men."   (What does "he ascended" mean except that he also descended to the lower, earthly regions? He who descended is the very one who ascended higher than all the heavens, in order to fill the whole universe.) It was he who gave some to be apostles, some to be prophets, some to be evangelists, and some to be pastors and teachers, to prepare God's people for works of service, so that the body of Christ may be built up until we all reach unity in the faith and in the knowledge of the Son of God and become mature, attaining to the whole measure of the fullness of Christ. Then we will no longer be infants, tossed back and forth by the waves, and blown here and there by every wind of teaching and by the cunning and craftiness of men in their deceitful scheming. Instead, speaking the truth in love, we will in all things grow up into him who is the Head, that is, Christ. From him the whole body, joined and held together by every supporting ligament, grows and builds itself up in love, as each part does its work. (Ephesians 4:7-16)

For this reason, I remind you to fan into flame the gift of God, which is in you through the laying on of my hands. (2 Timothy 1:6)

Offer hospitality to one another without grumbling. Each one should use whatever gift he has received to serve others, faithfully administering God's grace in its various forms. If anyone speaks, he should do it as one speaking the very words of God. If anyone serves, he should do it with the strength God provides, so that in all things God may be praised through Jesus Christ. To him be the glory and the power for ever and ever. Amen. (1 Peter 4:7-11)

CHAPTER SEVEN

The "it" of Lack of Wisdom

DEFINITION: Godly wisdom is the ability to understand what others cannot understand. It is knowledge of what is right, proper, and reasonable according to God's Word. It is using good sense and judgment. Lack of Godly wisdom results in bad decisions and living a sinful lifestyle.

FACTS ABOUT WISDOM:

There are two types of wisdom. The wisdom of God that comes from above and the wisdom of this world. James explains: *"Who is wise and understanding among you? Let him show it by his good life, by deeds done in the humility that comes from wisdom. But if you harbor bitter envy and selfish ambition in your hearts, do not boast about it or deny the truth. Such "wisdom" does not come down from heaven but is earthly, unspiritual, of the devil. For where you have envy and selfish ambition, there you find disorder and every evil practice. But the wisdom that comes from heaven is first of all pure; then peace-loving, considerate, submissive, full of mercy and good fruit, impartial and sincere. Peacemakers who sow in peace raise a harvest of righteousness."* *(James 3:13-18)*

Wisdom can be developed in three ways. Experience, observation, and revelation. Through your own experiences and by observing the experiences of others you can learn what to do and what not to do! The best way to learn, however, is through divine revelation from God and His written Word.

God is the one who gives wisdom. From the beginning of Old Testament record, God gave wisdom to His people to accomplish His purposes (Exodus 36:1-1; Deuteronomy 34:9; 1 Kings 4:19-30; Daniel 1:20; Acts 7:9-10.)

DEALING WITH WISDOM:

Repent of any unwise decisions you have made. This will give you a fresh start at living your life with the wisdom given by God instead of your own misguided wisdom or unsound guidance given by others.

Ask God for wisdom. Solomon asked for wisdom and received it (2 Chronicles 1:10-12). James advised: *"If any of you lacks wisdom, he should ask God, who gives generously to all without finding fault, and it will be given to him. But when he asks, he must believe and not doubt, because he who doubts is like a wave of the sea, blown and tossed by the wind. That man should not think he will receive anything from the Lord; he is a double-minded man, unstable in all he does"* *(James 1:4-8).* Proverbs 2:1-6 chronicles the intensity with which you should seek God's wisdom.

Learn from observation. You can learn from observing the experiences of others. In referring to the Old Testament record, the Apostle Paul said: *"These things happened to them as examples and were written down as warnings for us, on whom the fulfillment of the ages has come"* (1 Corinthians 10:11). He also advised: *"Join with others in following my example, brothers, and take note of those who live according to the pattern we gave you"* (Philippians 3:17). It is better to learn from observing others than experiencing negative circumstances yourself.

WHAT GOD'S WORD SAYS ABOUT WISDOM:

It is the spirit in a man, the breath of the Almighty, that gives him understanding. (Job 32:8)

Teach us to number our days aright, that we may gain a heart of wisdom. (Psalms 90:12)

Whoever is wise, let him heed these things and consider the great love of the Lord. (Psalm 107:43)

The fear of the Lord is the beginning of wisdom; all who follow his precepts have good understanding. To him belongs eternal praise. (Psalms 111:10)

Teach me knowledge and good judgment, for I believe in your commands. (Psalm 119:66)

My son, if you accept my words and store up my commands within you, turning your ear to wisdom and applying your heart to understanding, and if you call out for insight and cry aloud for understanding, and if you look for it as for silver and search for it as for hidden treasure, then you will understand the fear of the Lord and find the knowledge of God. For the Lord gives wisdom, and from his mouth come knowledge and understanding. (Proverbs 2:1-6)

Wisdom will save you from the ways of wicked men, from men whose words are perverse, who leave the straight paths to walk in dark ways, who delight in doing wrong and rejoice in the perverseness of evil, whose paths are crooked and who are devious in their ways. (Proverbs 2:12-15)

Blessed is the man who finds wisdom, the man who gains understanding, for she is more profitable than silver and yields better returns than gold. She is more precious than rubies; nothing you desire can compare with her. (Proverbs 3:13-15)

Wisdom is the principal thing; Therefore, get wisdom. And in all your getting, get understanding. (Proverbs 4:7, NKJV)

For whoever finds me [Wisdom] finds life and receives favor from the Lord. But whoever fails to find me harms himself; all who hate me love death. (Proverbs 8:35-36)

The way of the fool seems right to him, but a wise man listens to advice. (Proverbs 12:15)

Stay away from a foolish man, for you will not find knowledge on his lips. (Proverbs 14:7)

How much better to get wisdom than gold, to choose understanding rather than silver! (Proverbs 16:16)

A fool's mouth is his undoing, and his lips are a snare to his soul. (Proverbs 18:7)

He who gets wisdom loves his own soul; he who cherishes understanding prospers. (Proverbs 19:8)

Wisdom is sweet to your soul; if you find it, there is a future hope for you, and your hope will not be cut off. (Proverbs 24:14)

Wisdom is a shelter as money is a shelter, but the advantage of knowledge is this: that wisdom preserves the life of its possessor. (Ecclesiastes 7:12)

Wisdom makes one wise man more powerful than ten rulers in a city. (Ecclesiastes 7:19)

The wise will be put to shame; they will be dismayed and trapped. Since they have rejected the word of the Lord, what kind of wisdom do they have? (Jeremiah 8:9)

This is what the Lord says: "Let not the wise man boast of his wisdom or the strong man boast of his strength or the rich man boast of his riches, but let him who boasts boast about this: that he understands and knows me, that I am the Lord, who exercises kindness, justice and righteousness on earth, for in these I delight," declares the Lord. (Jeremiah 9:23-24)

Where is the wise man? Where is the scholar? Where is the philosopher of this age? Has not God made foolish the wisdom of the world? (1 Corinthians 1:20)

... but to those whom God has called, both Jews and Greeks, Christ the power of God and the wisdom of God. For the foolishness of God is wiser than man's wisdom, and the weakness of God is stronger than man's strength. Brothers, think of what you were when you were called. Not many of you were wise by human standards; not many were influential; not many were of noble birth. But God chose the foolish things of the world to shame the wise; God chose the weak things of the world to shame the strong. He chose the lowly things of this world and the despised things--and the things that are not--to nullify the things that are, so that no one may boast before him. (1 Corinthians 1:24-29)

This is what we speak, not in words taught us by human wisdom but in words taught by the Spirit, expressing spiritual truths in spiritual words. The man without the Spirit does not accept the things that come from the Spirit of God, for they are foolishness to him, and he cannot understand them, because they are spiritually discerned. The spiritual man makes judgments about all things, but he himself is not subject to any man's judgment: For who has known the mind of the Lord that he may instruct him? But we have the mind of Christ. (1 Corinthians 3:13-16)

For the wisdom of this world is foolishness in God's sight. As it is written: "He catches the wise in their craftiness". (1 Corinthians 3:19)

These things happened to them as examples and were written down as warnings for us, on whom the fulfillment of the ages has come. (1 Corinthians 10:11)

I keep asking that the God of our Lord Jesus Christ, the glorious Father, may give you the Spirit of wisdom and revelation, so that you may know him better. (Ephesians 1:17)

For this reason, since the day we heard about you, we have not stopped praying for you and asking God to fill you with the knowledge of his will through all spiritual wisdom and understanding. (Colossians 1:9)

If any of you lacks wisdom, he should ask God, who gives generously to all without finding fault, and it will be given to him. But when he asks, he must believe and not doubt, because he who doubts is like a wave of the sea, blown and tossed by the wind. That man should not think he will receive anything from the Lord; he is a double-minded man, unstable in all he does. (James 1:4-8)

The wisdom of God that comes from above and the wisdom of this world: Who is wise and understanding among you? Let him show it by his good life, by deeds done in the humility that comes from wisdom. But if you harbor bitter envy and selfish ambition in your hearts, do not boast about it or deny the truth. Such "wisdom" does not come down from heaven but is earthly, unspiritual, of the devil. For where you have envy and selfish ambition, there you find disorder and every evil practice. But the wisdom that comes from heaven is first of all pure; then peace-loving, considerate, submissive, full of mercy and good fruit, impartial and sincere. Peacemakers who sow in peace raise a harvest of righteousness. (James 3:13-18)

The book of Proverbs says more about wisdom than any other book in the Bible. That is the purpose of the book declared in Proverbs chapter 1. Read through Proverbs and mark all the references to "wise" and "wisdom."

CHAPTER EIGHT

The "it" of Lack of the Fruit of the Spirit

DEFINITION: The fruit of the Holy Spirit refers to the nature of the Spirit revealed in the life of the believer, spiritual qualities which should be evident in the lives of all Christians.

FACTS ABOUT THE FRUIT OF THE SPIRIT:

Spiritual Fruit comes through the Holy Spirit. It is the "Fruit of the Spirit", not the fruit of self-effort. Developing spiritual fruit is a continuing work of the Holy Spirit in your life as a believer to conform you to the image of Christ. Like fruit in the natural world, you must continue to cultivate it.

Spiritual Fruit is evidence of spiritual maturity. Like fruit in the natural world, spiritual fruit it is a product resulting from the process of life. It is Christian character that is manifested in both personal and social conduct and is the evidence of the Holy Spirit at work in your life. Just as fruit takes time to develop in the natural world, spiritual fruit also takes time to develop. It is the product of growth in the life of the Spirit.

Spiritual Fruit is singular. The word "fruit" is singular. It is not plural. Spiritual fruit can be understood by the natural example of grapes. A cluster of grapes has individual grapes on it, but it is one cluster. In the natural world, when grapes are picked from the vine they are picked in a cluster. This cluster of grapes is called the "fruit" [singular] of the vine. Spiritually, there is one cluster of fruit with many individual facets.

You are chosen to bear fruit. Jesus said: *"You did not choose me, but I chose you and appointed you to go and bear fruit--fruit that will last" (John 15:16).*

Jesus placed great emphasis on fruit bearing. Read the parable of the vineyard that did not yield fruit (Luke 13:6-9) and the fig tree which had no fruit (Matthew 21:18-19).

The Fruit of the Holy Spirit consists of these qualities.

-Love, an emotion of deep affection, care, and concern, an unconditional giving of self to others.

-Joy, a quality of gladness, delight, and jubilance. Happiness depends on the world around you and your circumstances. Joy originates with the Spirit of God and is not dependent upon what is going on in the world or your outward circumstances.

-Peace, a condition of quiet, calm, tranquility, and harmony. Peace is the absence of strife, anxiety, and concern.

-Longsuffering is the quality of patience, the ability to cheerfully bear an unbearable situation and patiently endure.
-Gentleness is the quality of having a mild manner that is not severe, violent, or loud. It is a

52

quiet and respectful kindness.

-Goodness, which is demonstrated through holiness and righteousness.

-Faith, a strong confidence in God which is manifested through a lifestyle of godly works.

-Meekness, which is controlled strength.

-Temperance, which is self-control, moderation in emotions, thoughts, and actions.

Developing the Fruit of the Spirit. Jesus used the term "fruit" of the Spirit as a natural parallel of a spiritual truth. Certain conditions are necessary to produce fruit in the natural world that are symbolic of things necessary for production of spiritual fruit. In the natural world, as well as the spiritual realm, specific conditions are necessary to assure growth. These include:

-Life: Just as life in the natural world comes through seed, life in the spiritual world came through the Seed of Jesus Christ (Genesis 3:15).

-Water: Water is necessary to produce fruit in the natural world and the water of the Holy Spirit is necessary to produce fruit in the spirit world. It quenches your spiritual thirst and brings spiritual growth (John 7:38-39 and Isaiah 44:3).

-Light: It is response to light that stimulates growth in the natural fruit bearing process. It is your response to the light of God's Word that produces the fruit of the Spirit (1 John 1:5-7).

-Air: Carbon dioxide is drawn in by a plant from the air which surrounds it and is necessary for growth and fruit production. The Word of God compares the Holy Spirit to air or wind (John 3:8). The "wind" of the Holy Spirit blowing across your life is much like the wind in the natural world. It scatters the seeds of the Word of God, separates the wheat from the chaff in your spiritual life, and fans the dying coals of your spiritual zeal to set you ablaze for God.

-Space: In Matthew 13 in the parable of the sower, competition for space choked out some plants. The believer who develops spiritual fruit will discover he must be set apart from the competition of the "weeds" of the world (Matthew 13:22; Romans 12:1-2).

-Roots: Roots are necessary to anchor and supply nutrients to the plant. Psalms chapter explains how to develop the root system in your spiritual life.

-Rest: Dormancy (rest) occupies a specific season in the natural growth cycle of plants. Dormancy is a period during which the plant may appear to be dead because there is no growth. Dormancy usually occurs right before a period of very rapid growth. One of the purposes of the baptism of the Holy Spirit is to bring spiritual rest and refreshing. This spiritual refreshing results in rapid growth of the fruit of the Holy Spirit (Isaiah 28:11-12).

-Soil: Both in the natural and spiritual worlds, in order to produce fruit the ground must be properly prepared. In the parable of the sower in Matthew 13 it was the condition of the soil that affected the growth of the seed. Your heart is like soil in the natural world. If your heart is hard and filled with things of the world that choke out the Word of God, you will not bear spiritual fruit (Hosea 10:12).

-Death: Every time you plant a seed to produce fruit, it does not come to life unless it dies first (John 12:24; 1 Corinthians 15:36). Spiritual life depends on death to the things of the world. It requires death to sin, worldly desires, and pleasures. Death to the world results in the development of the fruit of Christ-likeness in your life.

-Attachment to the vine: In order to bear fruit in the natural world, a branch must be attached to the main plant. If the branch is broken off from the main, life-giving vine it will not bear fruit. Jesus is the vine and we are the branches. In order to bear spiritual fruit, we must maintain our relationship to Him (John 15:1-5).

-Pruning: Pruning is necessary in the natural world if a plant is to remain productive and bear fruit. When a farmer prunes a plant, he cuts off the unproductive branches in order to make the plant produce more fruit. He removes everything which would hinder the growth of the plant. Pruning is also necessary in the spiritual world. Spiritual pruning is correction by God. The Bible also calls it chastisement. When God "prunes", He removes from your life everything which would hinder your spiritual growth. This process is necessary if you are to bear spiritual fruit (John 15:2).

-Climate: Climate is important in developing good fruit. In the natural world, many types of fruit are developed in environments that are specially controlled. They are grown in buildings called "hot houses" at specific temperatures. They are protected from the real environment of the outside world. If you take a "hot house" plant and move it outside, it will soon die because it has lived only in a controlled environment and it cannot withstand the environment of the real world. Spiritually speaking, we do not want "hot house" Christians who look good in controlled settings but wilt on contact with the real world.   Spiritual fruit should be just as evident in your contacts with the world as in the controlled settings of Christian friends and the church.

DEALING WITH THE FRUIT OF THE SPIRIT:

Analyze your life. Which manifestations of the Fruit of the Spirit are apparent? Which are lacking? Which need to be strengthened?

Rely on the power of the Holy Spirit that dwells within you. The Fruit of the Spirit does not develop through self-effort. It develops from the resident power of the Holy Spirit within you. The Holy Spirit works with you by convicting you when you violate scriptural principles that will impede your spiritual growth.

Provide the proper environment for spiritual growth. Review the conditions for developing spiritual fruit in the preceding section and make sure you are providing a proper environment for fruit-bearing.

Remember that fruit-bearing is a process. In the natural world as well as the spiritual world, fruit develops over time with proper care.   Do not become discouraged if you don't always seem to manifest the spiritual qualities of the Holy Spirit in challenging situations. Ask God for forgiveness when you fail, and then ask Him to strengthen you in the areas in which you are weak.

WHAT GOD'S WORD SAYS ABOUT THE FRUIT OF THE SPIRIT:

He is like a tree planted by streams of water, which yields its fruit in season and whose leaf does not wither. Whatever he does prospers. (Psalm 1:3)

The fruit of the righteous is a tree of life, and he who wins souls is wise (Proverbs 11:30)

Produce fruit in keeping with repentance. (Matthew 3:8)

Even so, every good tree bears good fruit, but a bad tree bears bad fruit.   A good tree cannot bear bad fruit, nor can a bad tree bear good fruit. Every tree that does not bear good fruit is cut down and thrown into the fire. Therefore, by their fruits you will know them. (Matthew 7:17-20)

"Make a tree good and its fruit will be good, or make a tree bad and its fruit will be bad, for a tree is recognized by its fruit." (Matthew 12:33)

The seed that fell among thorns stands for those who hear, but as they go on their way they are choked by life's worries, riches and pleasures, and they do not mature. But the seed on good soil stands for those with a noble and good heart, who hear the word, retain it, and by persevering produce a crop. (Luke 8:14-15)

He also spoke this parable: "A certain man had a fig tree planted in his vineyard, and he came seeking fruit on it and found none. Then he said to the keeper of his vineyard, 'Look, for three years I have come seeking fruit on this fig tree and find none. Cut it down; why does it use up the ground?' But he answered and said to him, 'Sir, let it alone this year also, until I dig around it and fertilize it.   And if it bears fruit, well. But if not, after that you can cut it down.'"
(Luke 13:6-9)

I am the true vine, and my Father is the gardener. He cuts off every branch in me that bears no fruit, while every branch that does bear fruit he prunes so that it will be even more fruitful. You are already clean because of the word I have spoken to you. Remain in me, and I will remain in you. No branch can bear fruit by itself; it must remain in the vine. Neither can you bear fruit unless you remain in me. I am the vine; you are the branches. If a man remains in me and I in him, he will bear much fruit; apart from me you can do nothing. If anyone does not remain in me, he is like a branch that is thrown away and withers; such branches are picked up, thrown into the fire and burned. (John 15:1-6)

You did not choose me, but I chose you and appointed you to go and bear fruit--fruit that will last. Then the Father will give you whatever you ask in my name. (John 15:15-16)

So, I say, live by the Spirit, and you will not gratify the desires of the sinful nature. For the sinful nature desires what is contrary to the Spirit, and the Spirit what is contrary to the sinful nature. They are in conflict with each other, so that you do not do what you want. But if you are led by the Spirit, you are not under law. The acts of the sinful nature are obvious: sexual immorality, impurity and debauchery; idolatry and witchcraft; hatred, discord, jealousy, fits of rage, selfish ambition, dissensions, factions and envy; drunkenness, orgies, and the like. I warn you, as I did before, that those who live like this will not inherit the kingdom of God. But the fruit of the Spirit is love, joy, peace, patience, kindness, goodness, faithfulness, gentleness and self-control. Against such things there is no law. Those who belong to Christ Jesus have crucified the sinful nature with its passions and desires. Since we live by the Spirit, let us keep in step with the Spirit. Let us not become conceited, provoking and envying each other. (Galatians 5:16126)

Do not be deceived: God cannot be mocked. A man reaps what he sows. The one who sows to please his sinful nature, from that nature will reap destruction; the one who sows to please the Spirit, from the Spirit will reap eternal life. (Galatians 6:7-8)

For you were once darkness, but now you are light in the Lord. Live as children of light (for the fruit of the light consists in all goodness, righteousness and truth) and find out what pleases the Lord. (Ephesians 5:8-10)

Through Jesus, therefore, let us continually offer to God a sacrifice of praise--the fruit of lips that confess his name (Hebrews 13:15)

CHAPTER NINE

The "it" of Lack of Love

DEFINITION: Love is a feeling of tender affection and devotion for someone. First Corinthians chapter 13 provides a complete biblical definition of love. The problems you may experience in the area of love are an inability to understand and receive God's love, love Him in return, and love others--including your enemies and the unlovable.

FACTS ABOUT LOVE:

God is a God of love. He loves you and loves through you. *"Whoever does not love does not know God, because God is love. This is how God showed his love among us: He sent his one and only Son into the world that we might live through him. This is love: not that we loved God, but that he loved us and sent his Son as an atoning sacrifice for our sins. Dear friends, since God so loved us, we also ought to love one another. No one has ever seen God; but if we love one another, God lives in us and his love is made complete in us"* *(1 John 4:8-12)*. Love originated with God (1 John 4:7). He shows His love by saving, healing, and comforting you and by supplying all of your needs. God even demonstrates His love when it is necessary to chastise and correct you (Hebrews 12:6).

Some people question why they suffer if God loves them. It is because we live in a sinful, fallen world where bad things happen. Just because you are a believer does not mean you are immune to adversity. You will not understand everything that happens to you (Deuteronomy 29:29), but God has promised to work all things--the good and the bad--together for your good (Romans 8:28). You also can develop positive spiritual virtues in times of adversity (1 Peter 5:10).

True love was not really understood until Calvary. The death of Jesus on the cross redefined the meaning of love: *"Greater love has no one than this, that he lay down his life for his friends"* *(John 15:13)*. God so loved the world that He sacrificed His Only Son to die for the sins of all mankind (John 3:16).

You love because you are loved. We love God because He first loved us (1 John 4:10).

Love identifies you as a true believer: Jesus commanded that you love others and said your love would identify you as a believer: *"A new command I give you: Love one another. As I have loved you, so you must love one another. By this all men will know that you are my disciples, if you love one another"* *(John 13:34-35)*. If you are hostile in your interactions with others, you are not demonstrating the love of God that should be the identifying characteristic of your life.

God's Word rests on the foundation of love. The entire revelation of God's Word rests upon this premise: *"Jesus replied: 'Love the Lord your God with all your heart and with all your soul and with all your mind.' This is the first and greatest commandment. And the second is like it: 'Love your neighbor as yourself.' All the Law and the Prophets hang on these two commandments"* *(Matthew 22:37-40)*.

The Bible says you must love others so that you can properly love God. *"We love because he first loved us. If anyone says, 'I love God,' yet hates his brother, he is a liar. For anyone who does not love his brother, whom he has seen, cannot love God, whom he has not seen. And he has given us this command: Whoever loves God must also love his brother" (1 John 4:19-21).*

Scriptures direct you to love your enemies. Jesus said: *"You have heard that it was said, 'Love your neighbor and hate your enemy.' But I tell you: Love your enemies and pray for those who persecute you, that you may be sons of your Father in heaven..." (Matthew 19:43-45).*

Love is the most important Christian virtue. It is a Fruit of the Holy Spirit that is to be manifested in all believers (Galatians 5:22). It is greater than any other spiritual quality in a believer's life (1 Corinthians 13).

Love is the opposite of lust. Love is a strong feeling of affection for another person, while lust centers on meeting your own personal desires. Love is a pure feeling coming from a pure heart. Lust is a passion for something that is wrong and comes from an evil heart. True love would never ask you to do something contrary to God's Word or anything that would be hurtful or violate your conscience.

You demonstrate your love for God by loving others (1 John 4:21); through devotion to His will and His Word (Psalm 40:8); time spent with Him in prayer (Jeremiah 29:12-14); and your service for Him (1 Corinthians 15:58).

DEALING WITH LOVE:

Confess your lack of love and your need for the love to God to be manifested in your life. Barriers to love include jealousy, pride, bitterness, hatred, unforgiveness, conceit, selfishness, etc. Search your heart and ask God to forgive these attitudes if they are present in your life.

Forgive those who have wronged you. This is the first step towards fulfilling the command to love your enemies.

Make a declaration that you will love God (Deuteronomy 6:5) and love others unconditionally (Matthew 19:43-45). Love is first an act of the will, not an emotion. Remember that confession is not only necessary for salvation, it is also required for other spiritual attainments as well. Just as you first confessed Christ and then learned to live a new life in Him, you must first confess your love for God and others and then learn how to live this love out on a daily basis.

Study 1 Corinthians 13. It is the most complete biblical definition of love. Ask God for these qualities of love to be manifested in your life.

WHAT GOD'S WORD SAYS ABOUT LOVE:

Love the Lord your God with all your heart and with all your soul and with all your strength. (Deuteronomy 6:5)

Love the Lord your God and keep his requirements, his decrees, his laws and his commands always. (Deuteronomy 11:1)

Hatred stirs up dissension, but love covers over all wrongs. (Proverbs 10:12)

You have heard that it was said, 'Love your neighbor and hate your enemy.' But I tell you: Love your enemies and pray for those who persecute you, that you may be sons of your Father in heaven... (Matthew 19:43-45)

Jesus replied: "'Love the Lord your God with all your heart and with all your soul and with all your mind.' This is the first and greatest commandment. And the second is like it: 'Love your neighbor as yourself.'   All the Law and the Prophets hang on these two commandments." (Matthew 22:37-40)

But I tell you who hear me: Love your enemies, do good to those who hate you, bless those who curse you, pray for those who mistreat you. If someone strikes you on one cheek, turn to him the other also. If someone takes your cloak, do not stop him from taking your tunic. Give to everyone who asks you, and if anyone takes what belongs to you, do not demand it back. Do to others as you would have them do to you. (Luke 6:27-31)

For God so loved the world that he gave his one and only Son, that whoever believes in him shall not perish but have eternal life. (John 3:16)

"A new command I give you: Love one another. As I have loved you, so you must love one another. By this all men will know that you are my disciples, if you love one another." (John 13:34-35)

As the Father loved Me, I also have loved you; abide in My love. If you keep My commandments, you will abide in My love, just as I have kept My Father's commandments and abide in His love.   "These things I have spoken to you, that My joy may remain in you, and that your joy may be full. This is My commandment, that you love one another as I have loved you. Greater love has no one than this, than to lay down one's life for his friends. You are My friends if you do whatever I command you. (John 15:9-14)

 Who shall separate us from the love of Christ? Shall trouble or hardship or persecution or famine or nakedness or danger or sword? As it is written: "For your sake we face death all day long; we are considered as sheep to be slaughtered."   No, in all these things we are more than conquerors through him who loved us. For I am convinced that neither death nor life, neither angels nor demons, neither the present nor the future, nor any powers, neither height nor depth, nor anything else in all creation, will be able to separate us from the love of God that is in Christ Jesus our Lord. (Romans 8:35-39)

Be devoted to one another in brotherly love. Honor one another above yourselves. (Romans 12:10)

For the commandments, "You shall not commit adultery," "You shall not murder," "You shall not steal," "You shall not bear false witness," "You shall not covet," and if there is any other commandment, are all summed up in this saying, namely, "You shall love your neighbor as yourself." Love does no harm to a neighbor; therefore, love is the fulfillment of the law. (Romans 13:9-10)

1 Corinthians chapter 13

 For all the law is fulfilled in one word, even in this: "You shall love your neighbor as yourself." (Galatians 5:13-14)

But the fruit of the Spirit is love, joy, peace, patience, kindness, goodness, faithfulness, gentleness and self-control. (Galatians 5:22-23)

But because of his great love for us, God, who is rich in mercy, made us alive with Christ even when we were dead in transgressions--it is by grace you have been saved. (Ephesians 2:4-5)

Be completely humble and gentle; be patient, bearing with one another in love. (Ephesians 4:2)

Husbands, love your wives, just as Christ loved the church and gave himself up for her (Ephesians 5:25)

Now about brotherly love we do not need to write to you, for you yourselves have been taught by God to love each other. (1 Thessalonians 4:9)

Keep on loving each other as brothers. (Hebrews 13:1)

Above all, love each other deeply, because love covers over a multitude of sins. (1 Peter 4:8)

How great is the love the Father has lavished on us, that we should be called children of God! And that is what we are! (1 John 3:1)

Dear friends, let us love one another, for love comes from God. Everyone who loves has been born of God and knows God. Whoever does not love does not know God, because God is love. This is how God showed his love among us: He sent his one and only Son into the world that we might live through him. This is love: not that we loved God, but that he loved us and sent his Son as an atoning sacrifice for our sins. Dear friends, since God so loved us, we also ought to love one another. (1 John 4:7-11)

We love because he first loved us. If anyone says, "I love God," yet hates his brother, he is a liar. For anyone who does not love his brother, whom he has seen, cannot love God, whom he has not seen. And he has given us this command: Whoever loves God must also love his brother. (1 John 4:19-21)

Everyone who believes that Jesus is the Christ is born of God, and everyone who loves the father loves his child as well. This is how we know that we love the children of God: by loving God and carrying out his commands. This is love for God: to obey his commands. And his commands are not burdensome. (1 John 5:1-3)

And this is love: that we walk in obedience to his commands. As you have heard from the beginning, his command is that you walk in love. (2 John 6)

CHAPTER TEN

The "it" of Deception and Dishonesty

DEFINITION: Deception and dishonesty refer to misleading someone and deliberately making them believe things that are not true. Bearing false witness against someone, cheating, and lying are synonyms.

FACTS ABOUT DECEPTION AND DISHONESTY:

Examples of deception and dishonesty include lying in business dealings, in relationships, cheating on tests or in financial matters, and deliberate misrepresentation of the facts.

Deception and dishonesty are common in politics and governments. Unscrupulous leaders say what you want to hear rather than tell the truth.

Deception is common in religion. There are many false teachers and cults that deceive multitudes of people around the world. The Apostle Paul warns: *"I urge you, brothers, to watch out for those who cause divisions and put obstacles in your way that are contrary to the teaching you have learned. Keep away from them. For such people are not serving our Lord Christ, but their own appetites. By smooth talk and flattery, they deceive the minds of naive people"* *(Romans 16:17-18).*

Deception and dishonesty are sin. One of the ten commandments addresses "bearing false witness", which means lying (Exodus 20:16). Leviticus 19:11 states clearly: *"Do not lie. Do not deceive one another."* Jesus repeated this command in Matthew 15:19; 19:18, Mark 10:19; and Luke 18:20. The Apostle Paul emphasized it in Romans 13:9.

God hates lying. Bearing false witness and a lying tongue are listed in Proverbs 6:19 among the top things God hates.

Satan is the father of lies. Jesus told the sinful Pharisees: *"You belong to your father, the devil, and you want to carry out your father's desire. He was a murderer from the beginning, not holding to the truth, for there is no truth in him. When he lies, he speaks his native language, for he is a liar and the father of lies"* *(John 8:44).*

Deception will increase in the end-times. The Apostle Peter warned about those who would scoff the Word of God and even say that the Lord was not going to return ((2 Peter 3:1-7). Timothy warns of "perilous times" in the last days, saying that men will be trucebreakers (dishonest) and that they will be *"ever learning and never able to come to the knowledge of the truth"* *(2 Timothy 3:17).* He also warned that these untruthful men would follow deceiving spirits and things taught by demons (1 Timothy 4:1-2). Jesus repeatedly warned believers to be on guard, lest we be deceived in the end-times (Matthew 24:4). One of the main characteristics of the Antichrist in the end-times will be deception. He will work "lying wonders" through the power of Satan and will deceive many people (2 Thessalonians 2:7-11).

DEALING WITH DECEPTION AND DISHONESTY:

Deception and dishonesty are sin. If you have been lying and cheating, you must recognize it is sin. As with any sin, you must confess this to God and seek forgiveness.

Accept and act upon the truth of God's Word. Ask God to put His Spirit of truth into your heart and mind (John 16:13). Put off the "old man" of sin which is corrupt and deceitful and put on the new self which is like God in true righteousness (Ephesians 4:22-23). Ask God to put a new heart within you, because bearing false witness comes from your heart (Matthew 15:18-19).

Ask forgiveness of those you have deceived. Be truthful and ask them to forgive you.

If you have a tendency to lie or deceive, make these verses your motto: *"Set a guard over my mouth, O Lord; keep watch over the door of my lips" (Psalm 141:3)* and *"Deliver my soul, O Lord, from lying lips and from a deceitful tongue" (Psalm 120:2, NKJV).*

If you have been lied to or deceived, forgive those responsible. Forgive them, but in the future deal with them as they are, not as you wish they were. Forgive, but unless they prove themselves to be trustworthy once again, do not place blind trust in them.

Ask God for the gift of discernment. This is a supernatural ability given by God to perceive the truth in any situation (1 Corinthians 12:10).

Immerse yourself in the Word of God. Feasting spiritually on the strong meat of the Word will enable you to discern between good and evil and truth and deception (Hebrews 5:12-14). The way to deal with deception is to learn the truth, then you will not be deceived.

WHAT GOD'S WORD SAYS ABOUT DECEPTION AND DISHONESTY:

You shall not give false testimony against your neighbor. (Exodus 20:16)

Do not lie. Do not deceive one another. (Leviticus 19:11)

You destroy those who tell lies; bloodthirsty and deceitful men the Lord abhors. (Psalm 5:6)

Who may ascend the hill of the Lord? Who may stand in his holy place? He who has clean hands and a pure heart, who does not lift up his soul to an idol or swear by what is false. (Psalm 24:3-4)

Whoever of you loves life and desires to see many good days, keep your tongue from evil and your lips from speaking lies. (Psalm 34:12-13)

You love evil rather than good, falsehood rather than speaking the truth. (Psalm 52:3)

But you, O God, will bring down the wicked into the pit of corruption; bloodthirsty and deceitful men will not live out half their days. But as for me, I trust in you. (Psalm 55:23)

For the sins of their mouths, for the words of their lips, let them be caught in their pride. (Psalm 59:12)

...the mouths of liars will be silenced. (Psalm 63:11)

No one who practices deceit will dwell in my house; no one who speaks falsely will stand in my presence. (Psalm 101:7)

Keep me from deceitful ways; be gracious to me through your law. (Psalm 119:29)

I hate and abhor falsehood but I love your law. (Psalm 119:163)

Deliver my soul, O Lord, from lying lips and from a deceitful tongue. (Psalm 120:2, NKJV)

Set a guard over my mouth, O Lord; keep watch over the door of my lips. (Psalm 141:3)

There are six things the Lord hates, seven that are detestable to him: haughty eyes, a lying tongue, hands that shed innocent blood, a heart that devises wicked schemes, feet that are quick to rush into evil, a false witness who pours out lies and a man who stirs up dissension among brothers. (Proverbs 6:16-19)

The integrity of the upright guides them, but the unfaithful are destroyed by their duplicity. (Proverbs 11:3)

Truthful lips endure forever, but a lying tongue lasts only a moment. (Proverbs 12:19)

The Lord detests lying lips, but he delights in men who are truthful. (Proverbs 12:22)

The righteous hate what is false, but the wicked bring shame and disgrace. (Proverbs 13:5)

A truthful witness does not deceive, but a false witness pours out lies. (Proverbs 14:5)

He whose tongue is deceitful falls into trouble. (Proverbs 17:20)

Better is the poor who walks in his integrity Than one who is perverse in his lips, and is a fool. (Proverbs 19:1)

A false witness will not go unpunished, and he who pours out lies will not go free. (Proverbs 19:5)

Better to be poor than a liar. (Proverbs 19:22)

Getting treasures by a lying tongue Is the fleeting fantasy of those who seek death. (Proverbs 21:6)

An honest answer is like a kiss on the lips. (Proverbs 24:26)

Do not be a witness against your neighbor without cause, for would you deceive with your lips? (Proverbs 24:28)

Like a club or a sword or a sharp arrow is the man who gives false testimony against his neighbor. (Proverbs 25:18)

Like a madman shooting firebrands or deadly arrows is a man who deceives his neighbor and says, "I was only joking!" (Proverbs 26:18-19)

A lying tongue hates those it hurts, and a flattering mouth works ruin. (Proverbs 26:28)

Keep falsehood and lies far from me. (Proverbs 30:7-8)

O Lord, do not your eyes look for truth? (Jeremiah 5:3)

Friend deceives friend, and no one speaks the truth. They have taught their tongues to lie; they weary themselves with sinning. (Jeremiah 9:5)

For by your words you will be acquitted, and by your words you will be condemned. (Matthew 12:37)

But the things that come out of the mouth come from the heart, and these make a man 'unclean.' For out of the heart come evil thoughts, murder, adultery, sexual immorality, theft, false testimony, slander. (Matthew 15:18-19)

...and many false prophets will appear and deceive many people (Matthew 24:11)

... Jesus said, "If you hold to my teaching, you are really my disciples. Then you will know the truth, and the truth will set you free." (John 8:31-32)

You belong to your father, the devil, and you want to carry out your father's desire. He was a murderer from the beginning, not holding to the truth, for there is no truth in him. When he lies, he speaks his native language, for he is a liar and the father of lies. (John 8:44)

O foolish Galatians, who hath bewitched you, that ye should not obey the truth, (Galatians 3:1, KJV)

You were running a good race. Who cut in on you and kept you from obeying the truth? (Galatians 5:7)

Then we will no longer be infants, tossed back and forth by the waves, and blown here and there by every wind of teaching and by the cunning and craftiness of men in their deceitful scheming. Instead, speaking the truth in love, we will in all things grow up into him who is the Head, that is, Christ. (Ephesians 4:14-15)

You were taught, with regard to your former way of life, to put off your old self, which is being corrupted by its deceitful desires; to be made new in the attitude of your minds; and to put on the new self, created to be like God in true righteousness and holiness. Therefore, each of you must put off falsehood and speak truthfully to his neighbor, for we are all members of one body. (Ephesians 4:22-25)

Let no one deceive you with empty words, for because of such things God's wrath comes on those who are disobedient. Therefore, do not be partners with them. For you were once darkness, but now you are light in the Lord. Live as children of light (for the fruit of the light consists in all goodness, righteousness and truth) (Ephesians 5:6-8)

Do not lie to each other, since you have taken off your old self with its practices 10 and have put on the new self, which is being renewed in knowledge in the image of its Creator. (Colossians 3:9-10)

Don't let anyone deceive you in any way, for that day will not come until the rebellion occurs and the man of lawlessness is revealed, the man doomed to destruction. He will oppose and will exalt himself over everything that is called God or is worshiped, so that he sets himself up in God's temple, proclaiming himself to be God. (2 Thessalonians 2:3-4)

The coming of the lawless one will be in accordance with the work of Satan displayed in all kinds of counterfeit miracles, signs and wonders, and in every sort of evil that deceives those who are perishing. They perish because they refused to love the truth and so be saved. For this reason, God sends them a powerful delusion so that they will believe the lie and so that all will be condemned who have not believed the truth but have delighted in wickedness.
(2 Thessalonians 2:9-12)

The Spirit clearly says that in later times some will abandon the faith and follow deceiving spirits and things taught by demons. Such teachings come through hypocritical liars, whose consciences have been seared as with a hot iron. (1 Timothy 4:1-2)

In fact, though by this time you ought to be teachers, you need someone to teach you the elementary truths of God's word all over again. You need milk, not solid food! Anyone who lives on milk, being still an infant, is not acquainted with the teaching about righteousness. But solid food is for the mature, who by constant use have trained themselves to distinguish good from evil. (Hebrews 5:12-14)

But there were also false prophets among the people, even as there will be false teachers among you, who will secretly bring in destructive heresies, even denying the Lord who bought them, and bring on themselves swift destruction. And many will follow their destructive ways, because of whom the way of truth will be blasphemed. By covetousness they will exploit you with deceptive words; for a long time their judgment has not been idle, and their destruction does not slumber. (2 Peter 2:1-3)

Dear children, do not let anyone lead you astray. He who does what is right is righteous, just as he is righteous. He who does what is sinful is of the devil, because the devil has been sinning from the beginning. The reason the Son of God appeared was to destroy the devil's work.
(1 John 3:7-9)

Dear friends, do not believe every spirit, but test the spirits to see whether they are from God, because many false prophets have gone out into the world. This is how you can recognize the Spirit of God: Every spirit that acknowledges that Jesus Christ has come in the flesh is from God, but every spirit that does not acknowledge Jesus is not from God. This is the spirit of the antichrist, which you have heard is coming and even now is already in the world. (1 John 4:1-3)

But the cowardly, the unbelieving, the vile, the murderers, the sexually immoral, those who practice magic arts, the idolaters and all liars--their place will be in the fiery lake of burning sulfur. This is the second death." (Revelation 21:8)

CHAPTER ELEVEN

The "it" of Unforgiveness and Reconciliation

DEFINITION: Forgiveness is the act of pardoning someone for an offense. Reconciliation is the ending of conflict between two or more people and the renewing of relationship. Included in the biblical concept of forgiveness is receiving forgiveness from God for sin, extending forgiveness to others, and forgiving ones' self. Forgiveness includes the releasing of grudges and bitterness over past offenses.

FACTS ABOUT FORGIVENESS AND RECONCILIATION:

Forgiveness and reconciliation come through Jesus Christ. *"All this is from God, who reconciled us to himself through Christ and gave us the ministry of reconciliation: that God was reconciling the world to himself in Christ, not counting men's sins against them. And he has committed to us the message of reconciliation. We are therefore Christ's ambassadors, as though God were making his appeal through us. We implore you on Christ's behalf: Be reconciled to God" (2 Corinthians 5:18-20).*

God promises forgiveness for your sin. When you confess your sins to God and repent, you are forgiven because He promises this in His Word (1 John 1:8-9). By repenting and accepting the sacrifice of Jesus Christ for your sin, you are reconciled to God. You may not "feel" forgiven, but the Christian walk is by faith not by feeling. God promised, and He cannot lie (Numbers 23:19).   Jesus said*: ..."whoever comes to me I will never drive away" (John 6:37).*

Broken relationships result in additional problems. Bitterness, grudges, resentment, anger, etc., all result from broken relationships. These negative emotions affect you mentally, physically, and spiritually. They are all sinful emotions that must be dealt with in order to receive and extend forgiveness.

The Bible teaches forgiveness. You need forgiveness from God and you are required to forgive others (Matthew 6:14-15). You also need to forgive yourself.

DEALING WITH FORGIVENESS AND RECONCILATION:

Be reconciled to God. A proper vertical relationship with God makes positive horizontal relationships with others possible. Confess your sins and ask God to forgive you. Read Psalm 51. You do not need to repeatedly ask forgiveness for a sin. Once you have confessed and asked forgiveness, God forgives and forgets (Isaiah 43:25). Remain reconciled to God by praying the model prayer, designed to be prayed daily, which includes "forgive our sins as we forgive others" (Matthew 6:12).

Repent of your unforgiveness. Repent of bitterness, anger, resentment, and holding grudges. These are all sin and must be dealt with as such.

68

Forgive others. You may not feel like it, but by an act of your will you must forgive others. Follow the directives given in Matthew 18:15-19.   Forgiveness is not:
-Justifying someone else's wrongs which they have done to you.
-Denying you were hurt in the first place.
-Accepting with resignation what was done to you.
-Waiting for time to heal the hurt. (It doesn't).

True forgiveness comes by:

-Recognizing what was done to you was wrong, the result of sinful men in a sinful world. It is not necessary to go back and relive the event mentally, but neither can you deal with it by denying it. Acknowledge what happened and how it affected you.

-Confessing the hurt to God and asking Him to heal you of the harmful emotions. You may never forget the facts of the incident, but what is needed is healing for the negative emotions relating to it.

-Asking God to help you forgive others, even as Christ forgives you. Recognize that God extends forgiveness to you as you forgive others: *"Forgive us our trespasses AS we forgive those who trespass against us."*

If others offend you again, forgive them again. Peter asked Christ how many times he was required to forgive someone. Jesus answered: *"I tell you, not seven times, but seventy-seven times" (Matthew 18:21-22).* He was actually saying that your forgiveness must be unlimited.

Forgive yourself. Distinguish between true remorse and guilt and shame. You are right to feel remorse, but guilt and shame are not from God. Jesus bore your sins, your guilt, and your shame on the cross (Hebrews 12:2). You do not have to bear these things (1 John 3:20). If you have confessed your sin to God and sought forgiveness and reconciliation with others, then you must also forgive yourself. See yourself as God sees you, a new creature in Christ (2 Corinthians 5:17). Here are some guidelines to help you forgive yourself.

-Acknowledge the sin that is causing your feelings of guilt. Confess your sin to God, and repent. Ask God to forgive your sin and heal your emotions.

-Recognize when God forgives, He forgets--He casts your sins as far as east from west (Psalm 103:12).

-Claim the promises of 1 John 1:8-9 and Romans 8:1.

-By an act of your own will, release yourself from condemnation. Control future thoughts by casting down "vain imaginations" of guilt and shame and "forgetting those things behind" (2 Corinthians 10:5 and Philippians 3:3).

WHAT GOD'S WORD SAYS ABOUT FORGIVENESS AND RECONCILIATION:

Blessed is he whose transgressions are forgiven, whose sins are covered. (Psalm 32:1)

Read David's prayer of repentance in Psalm 51.

For You, Lord, are good, and ready to forgive, and abundant in mercy to all those who call upon You. (Psalm 86:5)

He hath not dealt with us after our sins, nor rewarded us after our iniquities. For as the heavens are high above the earth, so great is his lovingkindness toward them that fear him. As far as the east is from the west, so far hath he removed our transgressions from us. (Psalm 103:10-12)

Hatred stirs up strife, but love covers all sins. (Proverbs 10:12)

He who conceals his sins does not prosper, but whoever confesses and renounces them finds mercy. (Proverbs 28:13)

"Come now, let us reason together," says the Lord. "Though your sins are like scarlet, they shall be as white as snow; though they are red as crimson, they shall be like wool." (Isaiah 1:18)

Forget the former things; do not dwell on the past. (Isaiah 43:18)

"I, even I, am he who blots out your transgressions, for my own sake, and remembers your sins no more." (Isaiah 43:25)

But he was wounded for our transgressions, he was bruised for our iniquities: the chastisement of our peace was upon him; and with his stripes we are healed. All we like sheep have gone astray; we have turned everyone to his own way; and the Lord hath laid on him the iniquity of us all. (Isaiah 53:5-6)

"Therefore, if you are offering your gift at the altar and there remember that your brother has something against you, leave your gift there in front of the altar. First go and be reconciled to your brother; then come and offer your gift." (Matthew 5:23-24)

Forgive us our debts, as we also have forgiven our debtors. (Matthew 6:12)

For if you forgive men when they sin against you, your heavenly Father will also forgive you. But if you do not forgive men their sins, your Father will not forgive your sins. (Matthew 6:14-15)

If your brother sins against you, go and show him his fault, just between the two of you. If he listens to you, you have won your brother over. But if he will not listen, take one or two others along, so that every matter may be established by the testimony of two or three witnesses. If he refuses to listen to them, tell it to the church; and if he refuses to listen even to the church, treat him as you would a pagan or a tax collector. (Matthew 18:15-17)

Then Peter came to Jesus and asked, "Lord, how many times shall I forgive my brother when he sins against me? Up to seven times?" Jesus answered, "I tell you, not seven times, but seventy-seven times." (Matthew 18:21-22)

The parable about forgiveness in Matthew 18:23-35 illustrates how your forgiveness by God is related to forgiving others.

And when you stand praying, if you hold anything against anyone, forgive him, so that your Father in heaven may forgive you your sins. (Mark 11:25-26)

But I tell you who hear me: Love your enemies, do good to those who hate you, bless those who curse you, pray for those who mistreat you. If someone strikes you on one cheek, turn to him the other also. If someone takes your cloak, do not stop him from taking your tunic. Give to everyone who asks you, and if anyone takes what belongs to you, do not demand it back. Do to others as you would have them do to you. (Luke 6:27-31)

Forgive, and you will be forgiven. (Luke 6:37)

All that the Father gives me will come to me, and whoever comes to me I will never drive away. (John 6:37)

A new commandment I give to you, that you love one another; as I have loved you, that you also love one another. By this all will know that you are My disciples, if you have love for one another. (John 13:34-35)

Repent, then, and turn to God, so that your sins may be wiped out, that times of refreshing may come from the Lord. (Acts 3:19)

Blessed are those whose lawless deeds are forgiven, and whose sins are covered; Blessed is the man to whom the Lord shall not impute sin. (Romans 4:7-8)

Therefore, since we have been justified through faith, we have peace with God through our Lord Jesus Christ, through whom we have gained access by faith into this grace in which we now stand. (Romans 5:1)

There is therefore now no condemnation to those who are in Christ Jesus, who do not walk according to the flesh, but according to the Spirit. (Romans 8:1)

All this is from God, who reconciled us to himself through Christ and gave us the ministry of reconciliation: that God was reconciling the world to himself in Christ, not counting men's sins against them. And he has committed to us the message of reconciliation. We are therefore Christ's ambassadors, as though God were making his appeal through us. We implore you on Christ's behalf: Be reconciled to God. (2 Corinthians 5:18-20)
In him we have redemption through his blood, the forgiveness of sins, in accordance with the riches of God's grace. (Ephesians 1:7)

...by abolishing in his flesh, the law with its commandments and regulations. His purpose was to create in himself one new man out of the two, thus making peace, and in this one body to reconcile both of them to God through the cross, by which he put to death their hostility. He came and preached peace to you who were far away and peace to those who were near. For through him we both have access to the Father by one Spirit. (Ephesians 2:15-18))

Be completely humble and gentle; be patient, bearing with one another in love. Make every effort to keep the unity of the Spirit through the bond of peace. (Ephesians 4:2-3)

Be kind and compassionate to one another, forgiving each other, just as in Christ God forgave you. (Ephesians 4:32)

For he has rescued us from the dominion of darkness and brought us into the kingdom of the Son he loves, in whom we have redemption, the forgiveness of sins. (Colossians 1:13-14)

For God was pleased to have all his fullness dwell in him, and through him to reconcile to himself all things, whether things on earth or things in heaven, by making peace through his blood, shed on the cross. (Colossians 1:19-20)

Therefore, as God's chosen people, holy and dearly loved, clothe yourselves with compassion, kindness, humility, gentleness and patience. Bear with each other and forgive whatever grievances you may have against one another. Forgive as the Lord forgave you. (Colossians 3:13)

See to it that no one misses the grace of God and that no bitter root grows up to cause trouble and defile many (Hebrews 12:15)

And above all things have fervent love for one another, for "love will cover a multitude of sins." (1 Peter 4:8)

If we claim to be without sin, we deceive ourselves and the truth is not in us. If we confess our sins, he is faithful and just and will forgive us our sins and purify us from all unrighteousness. If we claim we have not sinned, we make him out to be a liar and his word has no place in our lives. (1 John 1:8-10)

CHAPTER TWELVE

The "it" of Lack of Communication

DEFINITION: Communication is the act of giving or exchanging information through speech, writing, various forms of media and the arts, or through a common system of signs or behavior.

FACTS ABOUT COMMUNICATION:

The most important communication is that between God and man. God communicates through His Word and the gifts of the Holy Spirit such as prophecy and teaching.

The Holy Spirit communicates to convict us of sin (John 16:7-11) and to guide us into all truth (John 16:13).

Our primary mode of communication with God is prayer. In prayer, we speak with God and He speaks to us.

God has given you the ability to communicate. He has also declared that you will give an account on the day of judgment for every careless word you have spoken (Matthew 12:36).

Your tongue is powerful. The Bible says it has the power of life and death in it (Proverbs 18:21). Your own words can be a snare to your soul (Proverbs 18:7).

Your mouth, speaking God's Word, expedites the work of angels. The angels of God are released or hindered to work in your behalf by the words that come out of your mouth. Hebrews 1:14 reveals that angels are "ministering spirits" sent from God to minister in behalf of the heirs of salvation. They are released by God to minister when you speak God's Word instead of murmuring and complaining (Psalm 103:20).

The tongues is difficult to control. James 3:1-3 explains that the tongue is impossible to tame, apart from the Holy Spirit. The Bible compares the tongue to a fire (James 3:5); a world of iniquity (James 3:6); a beast that needs taming (James 3:7-8); a fountain of either fresh or bitter water (James 3:11); a tree bearing either good or evil fruit (James 3:12); an unruly evil (James 3:8); deadly poison (James 3:8); a sharp razor (Psalms 52:2); a sharp sword (Psalms 57:4; 59:7); a poisonous serpent (Psalms 140:3); and a deep pit (Proverbs 22:14).

What you speak comes out of your heart. If your heart is filled with negative thoughts--hatred, anger, jealousy, pride, bitterness, and strife--that is what will come out of your mouth. If your heart and mind are filled with carnal thoughts and lusts of the flesh, this will be manifested in your words. If your heart and mind are filled with positive thoughts--thoughts of faith, love, joy, peace--what you say will reflect this.

Controlling your tongues is mandatory because:

-You can be snared with your own words: *"You are snared by the words of your mouth; You are taken by the words of your mouth" (Proverbs 6:2, NKJV).*

-Your words can separate you from God: *"Who have said, with our tongue will we prevail; our lips are our own: who is lord over us?" (Psalms 12:4, KJV).*

-Your words can create a breach--an opening--in your spirit: *"A wholesome tongue is a tree of life: but perverseness therein is a breach in the spirit" (Proverbs 15:4, KJV).*

-Satan uses your lips to affect your soul: *"A fool's mouth is his destruction, and his lips are the snare of his soul" (Proverbs 18:7, KJV).*

-You tongue can cause calamity: *"He who guards his mouth and his tongue keeps himself from calamity" (Proverbs 21:23).*

-Your tongue affects your whole body: *"And the tongue is a fire, a world of iniquity. The tongue is so set among our members that it defiles the whole body, and sets on fire the course of nature; and it is set on fire by hell" (James 3:6, NKJV).*

-Your tongue affects your whole life: *"He who guards his mouth preserves his life, but he who opens wide his lips shall have destruction" (Proverbs 13:3, NKJV).*

DEALING WITH COMMUNICATION:

Ask God to forgive you. Evil communication is sin, and as all sin, must be dealt with by confession, repentance, and seeking forgiveness through Jesus Christ.

Get your heart right with God. The first step in gaining victory over the tongue is to get your heart right with God because..."*the things that come out of the mouth come from the heart, and these make a man 'unclean.' For out of the heart come evil thoughts, murder, adultery, sexual immorality, theft, false testimony, slander" (Matthew 15:18-20).* Your mouth speaks what is in your heart. If your heart is not right, your tongue will reveal it.

Recognize that you are responsible for the words that come out of your mouth, so take control! *"But I tell you that men will have to give account on the day of judgment for every careless word they have spoken. For by your words you will be acquitted, and by your words you will be condemned" (Matthew 12:36-37).*

Keep your words few and simple. The more you talk, the greater the opportunity to sin with your words. *"When words are many, sin is not absent, but he who holds his tongue is wise" (Proverbs 10:19)."* Jesus said: *" Simply let your 'Yes' be 'Yes,' and your 'No,' 'No'; anything beyond this comes from the evil one" (Matthew 5:37).*

Set a good example by your communications. Your conversation reflects on the Lord, so you should set a good example by what you say: *"... set an example for the believers in speech, in life, in love, in faith and in purity"* (1Timothy 4:12).

Think before you speak. Take time to think about what you are going to say. The Bible warns:

Therefore, my beloved brethren, let every man be swift to hear; slow to speak, slow to wrath. (James 1:19, KJV)

If you have played the fool and exalted yourself, or if you have planned evil, clap your hand over your mouth! (Proverbs 30:32)

The heart of the righteous weighs its answers, but the mouth of the wicked gushes evil. (Proverbs 15:28)

Even a fool is thought wise if he keeps silent, and discerning if he holds his tongue. (Proverbs 17:28)

Think on these verses before you speak.

The wise in heart are called prudent, understanding, and knowing, and winsome speech increases learning [in both speaker and listener]. (Proverbs 16:21, AMP)

The mind of the wise instructs his mouth, and adds learning and persuasiveness to his lips. (Proverbs 16:23, AMP)

A man has joy in making an apt answer, and a word spoken at the right moment--how good it is! (Proverbs 15:23, AMP)

A word fitly spoken is like apples of gold in pictures of silver. (Proverbs 25:11, KJV)

He who guards his mouth and his tongue keeps himself from calamity. (Proverbs 21:23)

He who guards his lips guards his life, but he who speaks rashly will come to ruin. (Proverbs 13:3)

Ask yourself these questions before you speak.
       -Will what I am about to say bring glory to God?
       -Is it the truth?
       -Is it fair to all concerned?
       -Will it be beneficial to all concerned?
       -Will it edify others?
       -Have I talked to the person I am talking about?
             -Is what I am saying a fact that needs to be shared or is what I am saying based on rumors and does not need to be said?
             -Is it absolutely necessary that I share this?

Separate yourself from those who cannot control their tongues.   The Bible warns: *"Stay away from a foolish man, for you will not find knowledge on his lips"* *(Proverbs 14:7)*. Do not hang out with them and allow them to pour their filthy, godless conversations into your spirit.

Learn the power of peaceful words. *"Through patience a ruler can be persuaded, and a gentle tongue can break a bone" (Proverbs 25:15).*

Recognize your tongue is a weapon. Your tongue is a weapon you can use to overcome the enemy instead of being defeated by him: *"And they overcame him (Satan) by the blood of the Lamb and by the word of their testimony..." (Revelation 12:11, KJV).*

Avoid these communication errors which the Bible warns against.

-Murmuring and complaining: Complaining is actually a form of rebellion against God. When the nation of Israel complained against Moses and Aaron, God said they were actually complaining against Him. When you complain, you are rebelling against the way He is doing things and the circumstances He is allowing in your life.   Rebellion is compared to the sin of witchcraft in the Bible (1 Samuel 15:23).   As He did with Israel, God will execute judgment against those who murmur and complain (June 15-16).

-Profanity: Profanity is language or behavior that shows disrespect for God, Jesus, or the Holy Spirit including misuse of their names. It is vulgar and irreverent language or behavior, including jokes or innuendos that mock that which is holy.

-Covetous words*: "Keep your lives free from the love of money and be content with what you have..." (Hebrews 13:5).* See also "covetousness" in this database.

-Idol words: *"But I say unto you, that every idle word that men shall speak, they shall give account thereof in the day of judgment" (Matthew 12:36, KJV).*

-Foolish words: *"The discerning heart seeks knowledge, but the mouth of a fool feeds on folly"* *(Proverbs 15:14).*

-Unprofitable words: *"Keep reminding them of these things. Warn them before God against quarreling about words; it is of no value, and only ruins those who listen" (2 Timothy 2:14)*

-Fables and commandments of men: *"Not giving heed to Jewish fables, and commandments of men, that turn from the truth" (Titus 1:14, KJV).*

-Evil about things you do not know: *"But these, like natural brute beasts made to be caught and destroyed, speak evil of the things they do not understand, and will utterly perish in their own corruption" (2 Peter 2:12, NKJV).*

-Flattering words: *"You know we never used flattery, nor did we put on a mask to cover up greed--God is our witness. We were not looking for praise from men, not from you or anyone else"* *(1 Thessalonians 2:5-6).*

-Vain words: *"They speak vanity every one with his neighbor"* *(Psalms 12:2, KJV)* .

-Proud words: *"...with their mouth they speak proudly"* *(Psalms 17:10, KJV).* See also "Pride" in this database.

-Enticing words: *"And this I say, lest any man should beguile you with enticing words"* *(Colossians 2:4, KJV).*   Enticing words are words that sound wise and plausible, but are not.

-Boastful words: *"How long shall they utter and speak hard things? And all the workers of iniquity boast themselves"* *(Psalms 94:4, KJV)* .

-Words that misuse God's name: *"You shall not misuse the name of the Lord your God, for the Lord will not hold anyone guiltless who misuses his name."* *(Exodus 20:7).*

-Cursing and bitter words: *"Whose mouth is full of cursing and bitterness"* *(Romans 3:14, KJV).*

-Lies: *"Let the lying lips be put to silence, which speak grievous things proudly and contemptuously against the righteous"* *(Psalms 31:18, KJV).*

-Malicious words against others: *"So if I come, I will call attention to what he is doing, gossiping maliciously about us"* *(3 John 10).*

-Backbiting words: *"...and has no slander on his tongue, who does his neighbor no wrong and casts no slur on his fellowman"* *(Psalms 15:3).*

-Words of discord: *"...one who sows discord among brethren"* *(Proverbs 6:19, NKJV).*

-Contentious words: *"A fool's lips enter into contention, and his mouth calls for blows"* *(Proverbs 18:6, NKJV).*

-Words of strife: *"You shall hide them in the secret place of Your presence from the plots of man; You shall keep them secretly in a pavilion from the strife of tongues"* *(Psalms 31:20, NKJV).*

-Devouring and deceitful words: *"You love every harmful word, O you deceitful tongue!"* *(Psalms 52:4).*

-Froward and perverse words: *"Put away perversity from your mouth; keep corrupt talk far from your lips"* *(Proverbs 4:24).*

-Mischievous words: *"They also that seek after my life lay snares for me: and they that seek my hurt speak mischievous things and imagine deceits all the day long"* *(Psalms 38:12, KJV).*

-Tale-bearing words: *"A talebearer reveals secrets, but he who is of a faithful spirit conceals a matter" (Proverbs 11:13, NKJV).*

WHAT GOD'S WORD SAYS ABOUT COMMUNICATION:

You shall not misuse the name of the Lord your God, for the Lord will not hold anyone guiltless who misuses his name. (Exodus 20:7, NIV)

You have tested my heart; You have visited me in the night; You have tried me and have found nothing; I have purposed that my mouth shall not transgress. (Psalms 17:3, NKJV)

Let the words of my mouth, and the meditation of my heart, be acceptable in thy sight, O Lord, my strength, and my redeemer. (Psalms 19:14, KJV)

Keep your tongue from evil and your lips from speaking lies. (Psalms 34:13)

I said, I will take heed to my ways, that I sin not with my tongue: I will keep my mouth with a bridle, while the wicked is before me. (Psalms 39:1, KJV)

"Whoever offers praise glorifies Me; And to him who orders his conduct aright I will show the salvation of God." (Psalms 50:23, NKJV)

Create in me a clean heart, O God; and renew a right spirit within me. (Psalm 51:10, KJV)

You love every harmful word, Oh you deceitful tongue! (Psalm 52:4)

Praise the Lord, you his angels, you mighty ones who do his bidding, who obey his word. (Psalm 103:20)

Set a guard over my mouth, O Lord; keep watch over the door of my lips. (Psalm 141:3)

Put away perversity from your mouth; keep corrupt talk far from your lips. (Proverbs 4:24) Hear; For I will speak of excellent things; and the opening of my lips shall be right things.

For my mouth shall speak truth; and wickedness is an abomination to my lips. All the words of my mouth are in righteousness; there is nothing froward or perverse in them. (Proverbs 8:6-8, KJV)

The mouth of the righteous is a fountain of life, but overwhelms the mouth of the wicked. (Proverbs 10:11)

When words are many, sin is not absent, but he who holds his tongue is wise. (Proverbs 10:19)

The lips of the righteous nourish many, but fools die for lack of judgment. (Proverbs 10:21)

The words of the wicked lie in wait for blood, but the speech of the upright rescues them. (Proverbs 12:6)

From the fruit of his lips a man is filled with good things as surely as the work of his hands rewards him. (Proverbs 12:14)

Reckless words pierce like a sword, but the tongue of the wise brings healing. (Proverbs 12:18)

The tongue of the wise commends knowledge, but the mouth of the fool gushes folly. (Proverbs 15:2)

A man finds joy in giving an apt reply--and how good is a timely word! (Proverbs 15:23)

The heart of the righteous weighs its answers, but the mouth of the wicked gushes evil. (Proverbs 15:28)

Pleasant words are a honeycomb, sweet to the soul and healing to the bones. (Proverbs 16:24)

Starting a quarrel is like breaching a dam; so drop the matter before a dispute breaks out. (Proverbs 17:14)

A man of knowledge uses words with restraint, and a man of understanding is even-tempered. Even a fool is thought wise if he keeps silent, and discerning if he holds his tongue. (Proverbs 17:27-28)

A fool's mouth is his destruction, and his lips are the snare of his soul. (Proverbs 18:7)

He who answers before listening--that is his folly and his shame. (Proverbs 18:13)

From the fruit of his mouth a man's stomach is filled; with the harvest from his lips he is satisfied. The tongue has the power of life and death. (Proverbs 18:20-21)

He who guards his mouth and his tongue keeps himself from calamity. (Proverbs 21:23)

A word aptly spoken is like apples of gold in settings of silver. (Proverbs 25:11)

Through patience a ruler can be persuaded, and a gentle tongue can break a bone. (Proverbs 25:15)

A fool gives full vent to his anger, but a wise man keeps himself under control. (Proverbs 29:11)

Do you see a man who speaks in haste? There is more hope for a fool than for him. (Proverbs 29:20)

Do not be quick with your mouth, do not be hasty in your heart to utter anything before God. God is in heaven and you are on earth, so let your words be few. (Ecclesiastes 5:2)

Do not let your mouth lead you into sin... (Ecclesiastes 5:6)

The words of the wise are as goads, and as nails fastened by the masters of assemblies, which are given from one shepherd. (Ecclesiastes 12:11, KJV)

Do not pay attention to every word people say. (Ecclesiastes 7:21)

The quiet words of the wise are more to be heeded than the shouts of a ruler of fools. (Ecclesiastes 9:17)

So shall My word be that goes forth from My mouth; It shall not return to Me void, But it shall accomplish what I please, And it shall prosper in the thing for which I sent it. (Isaiah 55:11, NKJV)

Simply let your 'Yes' be 'Yes,' and your 'No,' 'No'; anything beyond this comes from the evil one. (Matthew 5:37)

Men will have to give account on the day of judgment for every careless word they have spoken. For by your words you will be acquitted, and by your words you will be condemned. (Matthew 12:36-37)

As for you, you were dead in your transgressions and sins, in which you used to live when you followed the ways of this world and of the ruler of the kingdom of the air, the spirit who is now at work in those who are disobedient. All of us also lived among them at one time, gratifying the cravings of our sinful nature and following its desires and thoughts. Like the rest, we were by nature objects of wrath. But because of his great love for us, God, who is rich in mercy, made us alive with Christ even when we were dead in transgressions--it is by grace you have been saved. And God raised us up with Christ and seated us with him in the heavenly realms in Christ Jesus, (Ephesians 2:1-6)

You were taught, with regard to your former way of life, to put off your old self, which is being corrupted by its deceitful desires; to be made new in the attitude of your minds; and to put on the new self, created to be like God in true righteousness and holiness. Therefore, each of you must put off falsehood and speak truthfully to his neighbor, for we are all members of one body. (Ephesians 4:22-25)

Let no corrupt communication proceed out of your mouth, but that which is good to the use of edifying, that it may minister grace unto the hearers. (Ephesians 4:29, KJV)

Let all...evil speaking be put away from you... (Ephesians 4:31, KJV)

But now also put off...filthy communication out of your mouth. (Colossians 3:8, NKJV)

Don't let anyone look down on you because you are young, but set an example for the believers in speech, in life, in love, in faith and in purity. (1 Timothy 4:12)

That the communication of thy faith may become effectual by the acknowledging of every good thing which is in you in Christ Jesus. (Philemon 6, KJV)

My dear brothers, take note of this: Everyone should be quick to listen, slow to speak and slow to become angry, for man's anger does not bring about the righteous life that God desires. Therefore, get rid of all moral filth and the evil that is so prevalent and humbly accept the word planted in you, which can save you. (James 1:19-21)

Likewise, the tongue is a small part of the body, but it makes great boasts. Consider what a great forest is set on fire by a small spark. The tongue also is a fire, a world of evil among the parts of the body. It corrupts the whole person, sets the whole course of his life on fire, and is itself set on fire by hell. All kinds of animals, birds, reptiles and creatures of the sea are being tamed and have been tamed by man, but no man can tame the tongue. It is a restless evil, full of deadly poison. With the tongue we praise our Lord and Father, and with it we curse men, who have been made in God's likeness.   Out of the same mouth come praise and cursing. My brothers, this should not be. Can both fresh water and salt water flow from the same spring? My brothers, can a fig tree bear olive, or a grapevine bear fig? Neither can a salt spring produce fresh water. (James 3:6-12)

...be holy in all manner of conversation; Because it is written, be holy; for I am holy. (1 Peter 1:15-16)

For, whoever would love life and see good days must keep his tongue from evil and his lips from deceitful speech. (1 Peter 3:10)

If anyone speaks, he should do it as one speaking the very words of God. (1 Peter 4:11)

CONCLUSION

How to Get Rid of "it" though Personal Deliverance

When you understand self-deliverance, you will keep yourself from being bond; you will keep yourself healthy, physically and spiritually and be free from spiritual pollution. Every day, you will enjoy divine health and will not be spending your money on drugs and hospital bills.

Sometimes, there may not be a minister who is anointed and knowledgeable about deliverance to help you. Sometimes, you can be heavily attacked and the next service is about four days away. What do you do? You should never allow evil spirits to reside in your life. If you lack adequate time to do a self-deliverance in the mornings, after your quiet time, then, when you're having your bath, you could do it.

Whatever the causes of our spiritual afflictions, there are several proven steps we may try to help ourselves find freedom and healing. If these steps do not resolve your situation, then perhaps it is time to ask for help:

Step 1 — Conversion

Deliverance from any level of bondage, or harassment (collectively called, "spiritual afflictions") cannot be achieved without personal conversion. Deliverance from milder forms of spiritual affliction may often be achieved by the various acts of personal conversion—Acts of Contrition, Faith, Hope, Charity, and Consecration. "Prayer Acts" and other prayers, with fasting, and various devotions are often effective to drive evil spirits away:

So humble yourselves before God. Resist the Devil, and he will flee from you. Draw close to God, and God will draw close to you. — (James 4:7,8)

The first step, therefore, is make up your mind to live the Christ-life; or if already doing so, to persevere in living the Christ-life. This internal conversion, which is a conscious decision and determination to follow Christ and all of His teachings, precedes all other steps to deliverance. Without conversion to the Faith in Jesus Christ and participation in His family, the Church, deliverance, even if seemingly effective for a while, cannot be successful in the long run. It is the *"Truth"* that makes us free (John 8:31b), not prayers, rituals, counseling, or personal will in themselves. It is the confrontation with Truth that sends the demons running back to hell. This is why the method of Deliverance Counseling we use is called a *"Truth Encounter"*. As demons are confronted with the Truth, and as we are confronted with the Truth, of whom we are in Christ, we gain freedom. The foundation of all truth is Jesus Christ, who is Truth (John 14:6). Without our Lord Jesus Christ, we can never know truth or obtain it.

Some people believe they are unable to make a profession of faith in Jesus Christ. In such cases the person should ask God for help—ask Him for the faith that will save, deliver, and heal.

If we are willing to accept the gift of faith from God, our Lord will give it to us when we ask:

82

And I tell you, Ask, and it will be given you; seek, and you will find; knock, and it will be opened to you. For every one who asks receives, and he who seeks finds, and to him who knocks it will be opened. What father among you, if his son asks for a fish, will instead of a fish give him a serpent; or if he asks for an egg, will give him a scorpion? If you then, who are evil, know how to give good gifts to your children, how much more will the heavenly Father give the Holy Spirit to those who ask him! — (Luke 11:9-13)

Sincerely ask God for the faith that brings saving faith, the faith of conversion to the One, that is Jesus Christ, whom who declares:

I am the way, and the truth, and the life; no one comes to the Father, but by me (John 14:6) .... Come to me, all who labor and are heavy laden, and I will give you rest (Matthew 11:28) .... I will not reject anyone who comes to me (John 6:37) .... [rather] take my yoke upon you, and learn from me; for I am gentle and lowly in heart, and you will find rest for your souls. For my yoke is easy, and my burden is light (Matt 11:29-30)

Step 2 — Repentance

Essential to growing closer to God in faith, devotion, and love is to repent of those behaviors, desires, beliefs, and ideas that are sinful. The definition of sin is much broader than most people imagine. A definition of sin:

Sin is an offense against reason, truth, and right conscience; it is a failure in genuine love for God and neighbor caused by a perverse attachment to certain goods. Its wounds the nature of man and injures human solidarity. It has been defined as "an utterance, a deed, or a desire contrary to the eternal law."

Sin is an offense against God: *"Against you, you alone, have I sinned, and done that which is evil in your sight"* (Ps 51:4). Sin sets itself against God's love for us and turns our hearts away from it. Like the first sin (of Adam and Eve), it is disobedience, a revolt against God through the will to become "like gods" (Gen 3:5), knowing and determining good and evil. Sin is thus "love of oneself even to contempt of God." In this proud self-exaltation, sin is diametrically opposed to the obedience of Jesus, which achieves our salvation (cf. Phil 2:6-9).

We must repent of our sin, but repentance involves more than merely "turning away" from sin. Repentance must also renounce all that opposes God and all that He finds sinful. This includes renouncing Satan and his ways, renouncing personal sins, and renouncing all that leads us to sin. Some of the common sins and situations that interfere with deliverance include: involvement in non-Christian activities like the occult; persistent situational sins such as living together without marriage or remarriage without annulment of previous marriages; maintaining improper or problematic friendships; illegal activities of any sort; and sins that have become habitual such as pornography, masturbation, fornication, gossip, lying, stealing, etc.

The three greatest stumbling blocks to deliverance is Pride, Rebellion, and Unforgiveness and all the things that go along with those three sins. Repentance of Pride, Rebellion, and Unforgiveness is required to even hope for deliverance. Repentance also includes the firm amendment to avoid sin, and the near occasion of sin, in the future. Repentance requires a *complete* turnaround of our lives, a becoming a *"new man"*, so that...

...you should put away the old self of your former way of life, corrupted through deceitful desires, and be renewed in the spirit of your minds, and put on the new self, created in God's way in righteousness and holiness of truth. Therefore, putting away falsehood, speak the truth, each one to his neighbor, for we are members one of another...(thus) do not leave room for the devil (Eph 4:22-25,26b)

Step 3 — Confession

With faith and contrition of heart, repentance of mind, firm purpose to avoid sin and that which leads us to sin, we must now confess our sins before our God who is a God of forgiveness and mercy. This is a critical step that we will discuss at length.

The manner of our confession differs, but within our respective traditions, confession is required:

If we confess our sins, he is faithful and just, and will forgive our sins and cleanse us from all unrighteousness. (1 John 1:9)

... if you confess with your mouth that Jesus is Lord and believe in your heart that God raised him from the dead, you will be saved. For one believes with the heart and so is justified, and one confesses with the mouth and so is saved. (Romans 10:9-10)

"Confess your sins to each other and pray for each other so that you may be healed. The earnest prayer of a righteous person has great power and wonderful results" (James 5:16).

This confidant maybe one's pastor or another minister, or a trusted friend. We must be careful when choosing an "accountability partner." Since we will be revealing very private and sensitive information about ourselves, it is critically important to trust whoever we choose as a confidant to be discreet and to keep absolutely confidential the information we tell them.

There is wisdom in presenting oneself to an "accountability partner." Personal accountability is upheld when we confess to another person whom may hold us accountable for our actions. Confessing our sins to one another is a powerful way to break the bonds of sin in our lives. It is much harder to confess our sins to one another than to simply say, *"Lord, forgive me"*. While God is forgiving, of course, it is the demands of personal accountability before another human being that brings our confession into grounded reality that strengthens our commitment to turn away from sin in the future.

Religious ministers, psychologists, counselors, and others including the Deliverance Counselors of agency, are also bound either by law, ethical codes, or contract with the client (or bound by any combination thereof) to keep private and confidential all that is revealed to them. In addition, those in the ministerial and helping professions are usually trained in the ethics, legalities, and culture of maintaining confidentiality. They are use to keeping private the personal information of their patients and clients. Friends, on the other hand, may not have such training and may not be use to the culture of confidentiality. Thus, if one's confidant is not a pastor, or at least a minister, psychologist, or counselor bound by law and/or ethical codes, take care to ensure the chosen confidant understands thoroughly that he must keep private all that he hears and may not discuss it with anyone, not even with his spouse.

There is a great psychological comfort in hearing the words, "I forgive you" or the equivalent, "I absolve you of your sins." Our Father in heaven understands this psychological need. Thus, in His great love for us, He provided a way for us to hear those words in His name. It is God who ultimately forgives sins, but God, according to His sovereign authority chose to delegate this authority to His validly ordained priests. This power was given to the Apostles in John 20:22-23 and was passed on from them to those whom they appointed.

Our Father in heaven also knows and understands our need to be a family and for the family to come to our aid when we are hurting, to offer forgiveness when we fall, and to provide healing and strength to help us grow in faith. God forgives you when you appeal to Him with your heart-felt and sincere repentance and confession. Follow the tradition of your denomination and always offer a prayer for forgiveness as soon as possible after sinning. Then, in obedience to the Bible, seek accountability by confession to a confidant to complete your healing.

Step 4 — Removing the Greatest Stumbling blocks: Pride, Rebellion, and Forgiveness

We have already mentioned that the three biggest stumbling blocks to deliverance is usually Pride, Rebellion, and Unforgiveness. These three sins distance us from God. To draw closer to God we need to give up our pride, obey our Lord's teachings, and forgive those who hurt us.

In Deliverance Counseling we help our clients through exercises to locate pockets of pride and rebellion and to rid themselves of these sins with the help of God through prayer. Forgiveness, however, tends to be the most difficult, partly because of pride or even rebellion perhaps, but mostly because of deeply emotional issues surrounding the circumstances of the hurts someone has given us. Whatever the causes of our unforgiveness, deliverance is not possible until we can come to forgive, thus we shall discuss this topic at some length too.

The following guide is rather long, but this step is one of the most important. One simple MUST deals with Pride, Rebellion, and Unforgiveness if deliverance and healing is to be permanently possible.

Pride: Pride is the essential sin that leads to most other sins. It is the sin of Lucifer that led him to rebel against God resulting in his expulsion from heaven and becoming Satan.

Pride is a killer. Pride says, "I can do it! I can get myself out of this mess without God and without anyone else's helped." No, we can't! We absolutely need God, and we desperately need each other.

Pride also says "I know the best and most efficient way and how dare others get in the way of that" or "How dare things not go my way" or "How dare some person or something get in the way of what I want to do." Impatience is a factor of pride. Other ways impatience reveals our pride is getting impatient when we cannot find our car keys, or when we are late to a meeting, or if someone is driving too slowly for us on the hi-way, or when the computer acts up and interrupts our train of thought.

Impatience is the sister to Pride because it is caused essentially by our desire to have things our own way, in our own time, and according to our own preferences.

Pride is also the engine behind egotism (thinking more of oneself than one ought) and behind false humility (putting oneself down to be less than what one actually is). Pride is the force behind resistance to lawful and appropriate authority — whether that authority is a parent, teacher, police officer, government, employer, or the Church.

Pride is the basis of thinking of oneself as better than others, being pompous, and having contempt toward one's neighbors, employers, other family members, or the Church and her ministers.

Pride can also rear its ugly head in more subtle ways such as reluctance to apologize when we need to apologize, demanding our rights merely because it is our right, being inappropriately unkind or rude, jealousy, being quick-tempered, moodiness, brooding over wrongs done by others to oneself, depression and despair, or demanding that we are right about something, when indeed we are right about the issue, even though the issue is unimportant or can be handled differently (this is a major phenomenon in marriages, families, and friendships — the phrase "We need to choose our battles" is an important remedy for this).

Other ways that Pride expresses itself include: by taking personal credit for gifts or possessions and thus refusing to acknowledge that we have what we have by God's Providence; glorying in our achievements as if they were not primary a result of God's grace and divine goodness; by minimizing one's defeats; by claiming qualities that are not actually possessed; magnifying the faults and defects of others or dwelling upon the defects and faults of others.

James 4:6-10 and 1 Peter 5:1-10 reveals that spiritual conflict follows pride.

Examine yourself for these and any other attributes of pride and then pray:

Dear Heavenly Father. You have said that pride goes before destruction and an arrogant spirit before stumbling (Prov. 16:18). I confess that I have not denied myself, picked up my cross daily, and followed You (Matt. 16:24). In so doing I have given ground to the enemy in my life. I have believed that I could be successful and live victoriously by my own strength and resources. I now confess that I have sinned against You by placing my will before You and by centering my life around self instead of You.

I now renounce the self-life and by so doing cancel all the ground that has been gained in my life by the enemies of the Lord Jesus Christ. I pray that You will guide me so that I will do nothing from selfishness or empty conceit, but with humility of mind that I will regard others as more important than myself (Phil. 2:3). Enable me through love to serve others and in honor prefer others (Rom. 12:10). Amen.

Rebellion: We often place our confidence in the flesh not only with the "I can do it myself" attitude but each time we assert our own opinions above the teachings of Christ. It is a pride and a rebellion to say, "I want to do it my way" or "I want to think the way I want" without regard to the ways God teaches us to go and to believe. This is an arrogance that not only can get us into major trouble but also forms a major vulnerability for demons to come into our life.

Rebelling against God and His authority gives Satan an opportunity to attack. As our commanding general, the Lord Jesus Christ says, *"Get into ranks and follow Me. I will not lead you into temptation, but I will deliver you from evil."*

The Bible teaches us that it is the will of God for us to be obedient to parents, to civil government, to the Church, and to the pastors who are over us. We have two biblical responsibilities in regard to these authority figures: 1) Pray for them; and 2) submit to them. The only time God permits us to disobey those in authority over us is when they require of us an act or acquiescence in ways that are contrary to Church Law, Natural Law, or Divine Law.

Being under authority is an act of faith; we are trusting God to work through His established lines of authority. The authority that God has ordained does not mean, however, that we are to submit to abuse from those authorities. In those cases where someone in authority over us is abusing us in any way, then we need to act in appropriate ways according to the situation — such as appeal to the state for protection and relief for civil or criminal issues; or appeal to Church authorities on some issue involving religion or our parish; or make appropriate decisions such as terminating an abusive relationship, etc. Whoever the authority, who is abusing, we need to pray for the offender and to forgive him; but we are not required to be a doormat or target of their abuse.

Some of the lines of authority mentioned in the Bible include:

- Church leaders (Hebrews 13:17; Matthew 18:15-18)
- Parents (Ephesians 6: 1-3; Exodus 20:12)
- Husbands (1 Peter 3:1-3; Ephesians 5:23-24)
- Employers (1 Peter 2:18-21)
- Civil Government (Romans 13:1-5; 1 Timothy 2:1-3; 1 Peter 2:13-16)

Examine yourself for any areas of rebellion (deliberate driving faster than the speed limit is rebellion, too, you know!) and then pray:

Dear Heavenly Father. You have said that rebellion is as the sin of witchcraft and insubordination is as iniquity and idolatry (1 Sam. 15:23). I know that in action and attitude I have sinned against You with a rebellious heart. I ask Your forgiveness for my rebellion and pray that by the shed blood of the Lord Jesus Christ, strengthened by intercession of the that all ground gained by evil spirits because of my rebelliousness be canceled and taken back. I pray that You will shed light on all my ways that I may know the full extent of my rebelliousness, and I now choose to adopt a submissive spirit and a servant's heart. Amen.

Unforgiveness: Jesus Himself discusses the seriousness of failing to forgive. He tells us that failure to forgive those who hurt us will result in our not being forgiven ourselves by God. *"Forgive us our trespasses (sins) as we forgive those who trespass (sin) against us"*. The *Our Father*, the Lord's Prayer, which most all of us know and pray, Jesus teaches us that God will be as forgiving to us as we are to others.

Indeed, how can we expect God to forgive us when we do not forgive our brothers? Consider the follow teachings from Holy Scripture:

If you forgive those who sin against you, your heavenly Father will forgive you. But if you refuse to forgive others, your Father will not forgive your sins (Matthew 6:14,15).

But when you are praying, first forgive anyone you are holding a grudge against, so that your Father in heaven will forgive your sins, too (Mark 11:25).

If you forgive others, you will be forgiven. (Luke 6:37b)

Forgiveness is not about emotions and feelings. You can still be hurting, angry and upset and still decide to forgive. Forgiveness involves a mental decision, a decision of will, an act of your free will, even though you may not "Feel it".

The true nature of forgiveness:

1. **Forgiveness is not forgetting:** People who try to forget find that cannot. It is an unfortunate quirk of the English language with the phrase, "Forgive and forget". In actuality this phrase does not mean to "forget" in the sense of not remembering what happened; of course, we will remember. God says He will "remember our sins no more" (Heb. 10: 17), but God, being omniscient, obviously cannot literally forget. "Remember no more" means that God will never use the past against us (Ps. 103:12).

   To forget is really "to let go". We need to *"let go and let God"*. We let go of the past, but more importantly we let go of the hurt. As long as we do not forgive, as long as we do not let go, we allow the offender of our wounds continue to hurt us.

2. **Forgiveness is a choice not a feeling:** Since God requires us to forgive, <u>it is something we can do</u>. God will NEVER ask us to do something that is impossible for us to do; that would be cruel and God is a loving God.

   Forgiveness, however, is difficult for us because it pulls against our feelings and emotional hurts. Forgiveness is not about forgetting our feelings or our emotional hurts. We often will not "feel" like forgiving, but we must forgive anyway. As the Lord Prayer teaches us, God forgives us "as we forgive others". But how can God require this of us when we have been hurt so badly?

   God does not expect your feelings and emotional hurts to be healed overnight. He knows and understands our feelings and our hurts. He is a compassionate God and will help us to heal over time, as we are able. What God expects of us is not an immediate emotional healing, but a decision of will to forgive, a decision of will to trust Him to take care of the offender and to heal us, a decision of will to ask God for, and to commit to, being healed of our wounds.

3. **Forgiveness is not letting the person off the hook:** Forgiving is about you letting go, but it is not letting the offender off the hook. He will still pay for what he did, either before the Law or before God or both.

Forgiving is surely difficult for us because it pulls against our concept of justice. We want revenge for offenses suffered. But we are told never to take our own revenge (Rom. 12:9). Revenge does more damage to us than it punishes the offender. God's justice will prevail, no one can escape it. Never fear, those who hurt us will be held accountable, but we must let God deal with it. In order for God to deal with it, we need to let Him deal with it by letting go.

"Why should I let them off the hook?" But doing that is precisely the problem — we are still hooked to them, still bound by our past when we do not forgive.

To forgive does not mean letting the person off the hook; it means letting yourself off the hook.

4. **But you don't understand how much this person hurt me:** The problem is that when we do not forgive we, in essence, allow the person to still hurt us! The question is, "How do we stop the pain?" The answer is **to forgive!**

It is important to understand that we do not forgive someone for their sake; we do it for our sake so we can be free. Our need to forgive is not an issue between the offender and us; it is between us and God.

5. **Forgiveness is agreeing to live with the consequences of another's sin:** Forgiveness is costly. We pay the price of the evil we forgive. We are going to live with those consequences whether we want to or not; our only choice is whether or not we will do so in the slavery of bitterness and unforgiveness or with the freedom of forgiveness.

Jesus took the consequences of our sin upon Himself. All true forgiveness is substitution because no one really forgives without bearing the consequences of the other person's sin. God the Father *"made Him who knew no sin to be sin on our behalf, that we might become the righteousness of God in Him"* (2 Cor. 5:2 1).

Where is the justice? We might ask. It is the Cross that makes forgiveness legally and morally right: *"For the death that He died, He died to sin, once for all"* (Rom. 6: 10). This doesn't mean that we tolerate sin. We must always stand against sin, but we must give the offender to God and get on with our life.

6. **How do we forgive from our heart?** First, we acknowledge the hurt and the hate. If our forgiveness does not visit the emotional core of our life, it will be incomplete. Many feel the pain of interpersonal offenses, but they will not

acknowledge it. Let God bring the pain to the surface so He can deal with it. This is where the healing takes place.

Do not wait to forgive until we feel like forgiving; we will never get there. Feelings take time to heal mostly <u>after</u> the choice to forgive is made and Satan has lost his place (Eph. 4:26, 27). Freedom is what will be gained, not a feeling.

7. **Summary of Points on Forgiveness:**
   - Forgiveness is necessary to have fellowship with God.
   - It is not forgetting.
   - It is a choice.
   - Letting the offender off <u>our</u> hook is what frees us.
   - The offender is not off God's hook.
   - God says, "Revenge is mine."
   - You must acknowledge the hurt and the hate.
   - Forgiveness means we are agreeing to live with the consequences of another's sin — which we have to do anyway.
   - The justice is in the cross.
   - Choice is between the slavery of bitterness or the freedom of forgiveness.
   - Forgiveness means not using the past against the offender.
   - Forgiveness <u>does not</u> mean tolerating the sin or abuse.
   - Why forgive? To stop the pain! As we live in unforgiveness the offender still hurts us!
   - The issue of forgiveness is between you and God only.
   - The act of forgiveness is for your sake, and for your freedom.

Think about the people in your life for whom you need to forgive, people to whom you hold bitterness, people who have hurt you or disappointed you in anyway, or for whom you hold any kind of grudge. Be sure to ALWAYS include your parents, siblings, spouse, and YOURSELF. There is always something to forgive in our families and in ourselves.

Record all the names you can think of on a sheet of paper and a brief note as to why you need to forgive them. If you do not remember names, list them by what you do remember, such as "the guy in sixth grade with the red hat". If you cannot remember why you need to forgive someone on your list that is okay; forgive them for whatever it was — God knows.

After preparing this list ask God to bring to your mind anyone you have forgotten. It is not unusual to forget, or to push aside from our conscious mind, incidents and even the names of people whom have hurt us. These hidden hurts and wounds need to be healed as well. Thus, ask God to bring to your mind any person you have forgotten for whom you need to forgive, for whom you hold a grudge against, for which you are bitter, for those who have hurt you, with the following prayer:

Father in heaven, please bring to my mind the names of any people for whom I have held bitterness towards, grudges against, or have not forgiven for the hurts they have caused me. Help me to remember all these hurts so that they may be offered to You, O Lord, and healed from my soul so that I may live the truly victorious Christ-life. Amen.

Add to your list the names of anyone God may bring to your mind.

Now it is time to pray...

The following prayer needs to be said for each person on the list for which you need to forgive. Do not go to the next person on the list until you are sure you have dealt with all the remembered pain.

As you pray, God may bring to your mind various offending people and experiences that has been totally forgotten. Allow God to do this even if it is painful. Remember this process of forgiveness is for your sake because God wants you to be free.

Remember also that by forgiving the offender we are not rationalizing or trying to explain the offender's behavior. Forgiveness deals with the victim's pain, your pain, not another's excuses. Positive feelings will follow in time; freeing you from the past is the critical issue now.

If you are willing to forgive for your sake, so that you can walk away from this webpage free in Christ, free from the past and from person who hurt you, pray the introductory prayer below and then pray the "Prayer to Forgive" for each person on your list:

Heavenly Father, I now ask for your help in forgiving all those people on my list. Although I am still hurt and angry with them, I know that they are your children and that you love them more than I can possibly know. For this reason, my God, I ask you to help me forgive them. I lay down all bitterness, resentment and hatred for this person and I freely choose to forgive them. Teach me to be more merciful, my God, and help me be always willing, just as you are always willing, to forgive those who sin against me. Amen."

Prayer to Forgive

Lord, I forgive _______________________________ for (specifically identify all offenses and painful memories).

May God heal you and bless you!

Step 5 — Know Who You Are in Christ!

In order to gain freedom, it is important to know who you are in Christ. Thus, you need to evaluate the concept you have of yourself, to acknowledge the truth about God and about yourself; about your relationship and ideas about God and about the manner of our lives.

We often deceive ourselves about our position in Christ and our relationship with Him. For example, we may say to ourselves: "This isn't going to work" or "I wish I could believe this but I can't" or perhaps even more direct deceptions or denials concerning the promises of God for His children. Areas of deception that we may have include:

1. **Self-Deception** (telling ourselves things that are not true)

- o Listening to God's words but thinking we do not have to do it (Ja 1:22; 4:17)
- o Thinking we have no sin or do not sin (1 Jn 1:8)
- o Thinking that we are something when we are not (Gal 6:3)
- o Believing that we will not reap what we sow (Gal 6:7)
- o Thinking we are wise and sophisticated in the 21st century (1 Cor 3:18, 19)
- o Believing that the unrighteous will reach heaven (1 Cor 6:9)
- o Thinking we can associate with bad company and not be corrupted (1 Cor 15:33)

2. **Self-Defense** (defending ourselves instead of trusting Christ)
- o Denial (conscious or subconscious)
- o Fantasy (escape from the real world)
- o Emotional insulation (withdraw to avoid rejection)
- o Regression (reverting back to a less threatening time in the past)
- o Displacement (taking out frustrations on others)
- o Projection (blaming others or accusing others of things we ourselves have done)
- o Rationalization (defending self though verbal excursion)

To counter these and other deceptions we tell ourselves we need to exercise faith. Faith is the response to Truth and believing the truth is a CHOICE (not a feeling). If we say, "I want to believe God, but I just can't," then we are deceiving ourselves. Of course, we can believe God. We know that God does not lie. Faith is something we DECIDE to do; it is not something we FEEL like doing. Believing the truth does not make it true; rather it is TRUE, therefore we believe it.

Examine yourself and how you may deceive yourself with "self-deceptions" and "Self-Defense" mechanisms. The pray the following prayer: ...

Prayer to Know the Truth:

Dear Heavenly Father. I know that You desire truth in the inner self and that facing this truth is the way of liberation (John 8:32). I acknowledge that I have been deceived by the father of lies (John 8:44) and that I have deceived myself (1 John 1:8). I pray in the name of the Lord Jesus Christ, and since by faith I have received You into my life and am now seated with Christ in the heavenliest (Eph 2:6), I ask you Father to command all deceiving spirits to depart from me. I now ask You to *"search me, O God, and know my heart: try me and know my anxious thoughts; and see if there be any hurtful way in me, and lead me in the everlasting way"* (Ps. 139:23, 24) In the name of Christ Jesus I pray. Amen.

Knowing the truth about oneself, overcoming self-deceptions and the mechanism of self-defense that hide who we really are, includes understanding our faith in Christ. It is by Christ that our lives have meaning and substance.

The following prayer is the substance of that faith:

Affirmations

I believe that I am a child of God (1 Jn. 3:1-3) and that I am seated with Christ in the heavenlies (Eph. 2:6). I believe that I was saved by the grace of God through faith that is a gift and not the result of my own efforts or merits (Eph 2:8).

I choose to be strong in the Lord and in the strength of His might (Eph 6:10). I put no confidence in the flesh (Phil 3:3) for the weapons of warfare are not of the flesh (2 Cor. 10:4). I put on the whole armor of God (Eph. 6:10-20), and I resolve to stand firm in my faith and to resist the evil one.

I believe that Jesus Christ has all authority in heaven and on earth (Matt 28:18) and that He is the head over all rule and authority (Col 2:10). I believe that Satan and his demons and wicked spirits are subject to the Lord Jesus Christ and therefore to me in Christ since I am a member of Christ's body (Eph 1:19-23).

I believe that apart from Christ I can do nothing (John 15:5) so I declare my dependence upon Him.

I choose to abide in Christ in order to bear much fruit and to glorify the Lord (Jn 15:8) and to accomplish the work of sanctification that Christ began in me through the Cross (James 2).

I believe that since I am a member go God's royal family I have the authority, in the name of Christ Jesus, to ask the Father to command the devil to leave my presence, as I obey the command to resist the devil (James 4:7).

I reject any counterfeit gifts or works of Satan and his minions in my life.

I believe that the truth will set me free (John 8:32) and that walking in the light is the only path of fellowship and freedom (1 John 1:7). Therefore, as a royal member of God's household, I stand against Satan's deceptions by affirming all the doctrines of the Faith and by taking every thought captive in obedience to Christ (2 Cor 10:5).

I declare that the Bible and the Church are the only authoritative standards for me (2 Tim 3:15, 16).

I choose to speak the truth in love (Eph 4:15).

I choose to present my body as an instrument of righteousness, a living and holy sacrifice, and thus I renew my mind daily by the living Word of God in order that I may prove that the will of God is good, acceptable, and perfect (Rom 6:13; 12:1, 2).

I ask my heavenly Father to fill me with His Holy Spirit (Eph 5:18), to lead me into all truth (John 16:13), and to empower my life that I may live above sin and not carry out the desires of the flesh (Gal 5:16). I crucify the flesh (Gal 5:24) and choose to walk by the Spirit.

In making all these affirmations, I renounce all selfish goals and choose the ultimate goal of love (1 Tim 1:5). I choose to obey the greatest commandment to love the Lord my God will all my heart, soul, and mind, and to love my neighbor as myself (Matt 22:37-39). Amen.

Step 6 — Worship, Pray, and Fast

Worship as a Church Family: One of Satan's favorite lies, apart from having us believe that he does not exist, or that he does exist and is more powerful than he truly is, is that since God is everywhere and we can worship Him anywhere and do not need the "community of believers ", the Church family.

Although it is true that God is everywhere and worshiping Him anywhere is wholesome and good, it is false to believe that the Church is unnecessary. Since the earliest days of Christianity, communities of believers gathered together on the *Lord's Day* (Sunday).

Scripture is very clear on the subject of Church attendance and on how our submission to its authority is not only good but required. The Church, its leaders and members, are the Mystical Body of Christ here on Earth. To disobey the teachings of the Church as it relates to faith and morals is to disobey the teachings of Christ. To not attend church is also disobedience to Christ.

Paul admonishes those who do not come to Church in Hebrews 10:19-25:

Therefore, brothers, since through the blood of Jesus we have confidence of entrance into the sanctuary by the new and living way he opened for us through the veil, that is, his flesh, and since we have "a great priest over the house of God," let us approach with a sincere heart and in absolute trust, with our hearts sprinkled clean from an evil conscience and our bodies washed in pure water. Let us hold unwaveringly to our confession that gives us hope, for he who made the promise is trustworthy. We must consider how to rouse one another to love and good works. We should not stay away from our assembly, as is the custom of some, but encourage one another, and this all the more as you see the day drawing near.

Hebrews 13:17

Obey your leaders and submit to them; for they are keeping watch over your souls, as men who will have to give account. Let them do this joyfully, and not sadly, for that would be of no advantage to you.

Worship and prayer together as a family, prayer meetings, adoration, and other corporate settings, and in the privacy of the family at home is critical in developing spiritual health for the family and each family member. Such family devotion forms the foundation for all that each family does away from home in the world of school, work, and society.

Prayer is so important both in the family context and individually. It is important not just because prayer is something a Christian ought to do, but because prayer is communication.

The more we depend on God, the closer He is to us and we are to Him. Aligning ourselves with God, communicating with Him at all times and in all situations and personal decisions will unite our hearts to His. A heart united to the Creator will overflow with graces and blessings.

Prayer and Spiritual Warfare: In addition, a healthy prayer life destroys strongholds that demons may have in our lives and in our hearts. Without prayer we cannot hope to be delivered from spiritual afflictions. It is no secret —prayer, worship, devotion, and living the Christ-Life in all that it entails is the formula not only for deliverance from spiritual afflictions, but for living the victorious life in Christ.

When dealing with spiritual afflictions, however, some special prayer considerations may be needed. Scripture states that there are certain demons that will only respond to prayer as well as fasting: *"But this kind does not go out except by prayer and fasting."* (Matthew 17:21). If fasting can defeat even the strongest of fallen angels, just how powerful is this sacrifice that we can make?

Spiritual warfare prayers are very effective in defeating the enemy and drawing our hearts closer to God.

Step 7 — Live the Faith and Remain Faithful

Along with all the advice and recommendations of the first six steps, our healing and deliverance cannot be complete unless we act upon our faith. Doing good works and charitable acts of love are a natural outflow of our faith and necessary to lead a good Christian life. It is not enough to believe. James asks and admonishes in James 2:19,20, 26:

Do you still think it's enough just to believe that there is one God? Well, even the demons believe this, and they tremble in terror! Fool! When will you ever learn that faith that does not result in good deeds is useless?

Just as the body is dead without a spirit, so also faith is dead without good deeds.

James calls a man a fool who does not act upon his faith in James 1:22-25:

Be doers of the word and not hearers only, deluding yourselves. For if anyone is a hearer of the Word and not a doer, he is like a man who looks at his own face in a mirror. He sees himself, then goes off and promptly forgets what he looks like. But the one who peers into the prefect law of freedom and perseveres, and is not a hearer who forgets but a doer who acts, such a one shall be blessed in what he does.

It is hard to live the Christ-Life, but we must try. We must not have a faith that is dead and useless. We must not be a fool and not practice our faith. We must, rather, live out our faith and persevere in the faith:

1 Corinthians 9:23-27

All this I do for the sake of the gospel, so that I too may have a share in it. Do you not know that the runners in the stadium all run in the race, but only one wins the prize? Run so as to win. Every athlete exercises discipline in every way. They do it to win a perishable crown, but we an imperishable one. Thus, I do not run aimlessly; I do not fight as if I were shadowboxing. No, I drive my body and train it, for fear that, after having preached to others, I myself should be disqualified.

Colossians 1:17-23

He is before all things, and in him all things hold together. He is the head of the body, the church. He is the beginning, the firstborn from the dead, that in all things he himself might be preeminent. For in him all the fullness was pleased to dwell, and through him to reconcile all things for him, making peace by the blood of his cross (through him), whether those on earth or those in heaven.

And you who once were alienated and hostile in mind because of evil deeds he has now reconciled in his fleshly body through his death, to present you holy, without blemish, and irreproachable before him, provided that you persevere in the faith, firmly grounded, stable, and not shifting from the hope of the gospel that you heard, which has been preached to every creature under heaven, of which I, Paul, am a minister.

And thus, let us be able to say, with St. Paul, in 2 Timothy 4:6-8

For I am already on the point of being sacrificed; the time of my departure has come. I have fought the good fight, I have finished the race, I have kept the faith. Henceforth there is laid up for me the crown of righteousness, which the Lord, the righteous judge, will award to me on that Day, and not only to me but also to all who have loved His appearing.

Persevere in the faith and let your life be a living Gospel for you shall thereby *"know the truth and the truth shall set you free"*

I have outlined steps detailing certain issues that we have found important in gaining freedom for a person in spiritual affliction.

1. purify one's conscience by a good confession;
2. Receive Holy Communion as often as possible;
3. Implore the mercy of God by prayer and fasting.
4. Recourse to specific spiritual warfare prayers applicable to the situation.

Final Thoughts

Repentance, forgiveness, acting on our faith, praying, fasting, receiving the Sacrament frequently, and all the rest we ought to do as good Christians are very good things and very necessary for this life, but more importantly for the life to come.

The advice contained in these Steps to Self-Deliverance, however, are not "quick fixes". This advice involves a lifelong commitment for anyone with spiritual afflictions. Freeing yourself from the bondages of the enemy and keeping them from returning requires this commitment to persevere in Christ and in the Christ-life.

There will be dry times. Your faith will be tested. Indeed, the demons may (and more than likely will) try to return. Scripture speaks of what demons do once they are cast out:

Now when the unclean spirit goes out of a man, it passes through waterless places seeking rest, and does not find it. Then it says, 'I will return to my house from which I came'; and when it comes, it finds it unoccupied, swept, and put in order. Then it goes and takes along with it seven other spirits more wicked than itself, and they go in and live there; and the last state of that man becomes worse than the first. (Matthew 12, 43-45).

Do not leave your house (heart) *"unoccupied, swept and put in order"*; rather be filled with the Holy Spirit.

We can never let down our guard. As a final instruction, remember the teaching of St. Paul in Ephesians 6:10-18. We do not go about our day without putting on our clothes. Do not go into the world with God's armor:

Finally, draw your strength from the Lord and from his mighty power. Put on the armor of God so that you may be able to stand firm against the tactics of the devil. For our struggle is not with flesh and blood but with the principalities, with the powers, with the world rulers of this present darkness, with the evil spirits in the heavens. Therefore, put on the armor of God that you may be able to resist on the evil day and, having done everything, to hold your ground. So, stand fast with your loins girded in truth, clothed with righteousness as a breastplate, and your feet shod in readiness for the gospel of peace. In all circumstances, hold faith as a shield, to quench all (the) flaming arrows of the evil one. And take the helmet of salvation and the sword of the Spirit, which is the word of God. With all prayer and supplication, pray at every opportunity in the Spirit. To that end, be watchful with all perseverance and supplication.

APENDEX 1
Steps for Self-Deliverance

The purpose of all this information is to enable you to do a self-deliverance at home for yourself. The process of self-deliverance is carried out in stages. Let's go through them one by one.

STEP ONE: Start with praise and worship. You can sing songs to praise God and to worship Him.

STEP TWO: Confess out loud Scriptures promising deliverance. Luke 10:19, Ephesians 1:7, Romans 16:20, Revelation 12:11, Colossians 2:14-15, Galatians 3:13-14, Psalms 91:3…*2 Timothy 4:18* says And the Lord shall deliver me from every evil work, and will preserve me unto His heavenly kingdom: to whom be glory forever and ever. Amen. You should memorize *2 Tim 4:18*.

STEP THREE: Break covenants and curses to destroy their legal hold. You pray a simple prayer like this: I break any curse or covenant working against me, in the name of Jesus. (Simple prayers)

STEP FOUR: Bind all the spirits associated with those covenants and curses like this: I bind all the spirits attached or connected to the curses and covenants I have just broken, in the name of Jesus.

STEP FIVE: Lay one hand on your head and pray, Holy Ghost, cover me from the top of my head to the sole of my feet, in the name of Jesus. Begin to mention every organ of your body; kidney, liver, intestine, blood, etc. You must not rush at this level. Lay your hands-on areas that the Spirit of God leads you to.

STEP SIX: Then begin to saturate yourself with the Blood of Jesus. You do this by saying: I plead the Blood of Jesus over me. This must continue until you have a release in your spirit to stop.

STEP SEVEN: It is now, that you can demand firmly, in the name of the Lord Jesus Christ, that any spirit that is not of God should leave you. You demand it forcefully like this: In the name of the Lord Jesus Christ, I come against all you hidden spirits and I bind your activities in my life. You can no longer hide below the surface because I now recognize what you have been doing; release me, in the name of Jesus.

(**If sickness is the problem, address it and say**) You spirit of infirmity, I speak to you directly, get out of my life now. I am redeemed by the Blood of Jesus Christ, come out and go now. Go out with every breath by the power of the Holy Spirit. I prevail over you, in the name of Jesus.

98

STEP EIGHT: Ask for a fresh in-filling of the Holy Spirit and close the session with praises. Self-deliverance keeps you from getting sick; it removes every evil seed of the enemy; it charges your body with fire. It uproots evil plantations and builds up your confidence. Every night before you go to bed, you must remember these two important prayer points.

1. Pray for cover with the Blood of Jesus. ***Revelation 12:11*** = And they overcame him by the Blood of the Lamb, and by the word of their testimony; and they loved not their lives unto the death.
2. Pray that the Angels of God should surround you. ***Psalms 34:7*** = The Angel of the Lord encampeth round about them that fear him, and delivereth them.

No matter how sleepy you are, make sure pray these two prayer points every night. There is no reason why self-deliverance should not be effective. However, if the person seeking deliverance is under stubborn demonic control or hereditary strongman and lacks sufficient faith or authority to defeat the oppressors or living in any known sin, the evil spirits will be hard to get rid of. right.

One final word of caution. For a person to be delivered, he/she must want deliverance. Self-deliverance must not be done because of pride, shyness, the fear of possible public embarrassment, etc. Your motive for engaging in self-deliverance has to be pure.

REMEMBER: ***DELIVERANCE IS A PROCESS (((NOT A ONE-TIME EVENT)))*** AND THE LENGTH OF TIME IT TAKES DEPENDS ON SEVERAL THINGS;

1. The length of time the spirit has stayed inside a person
2. The strength and reinforcement of the spirit
3. The experience and degree of anointing upon those who are ministering the deliverance
4. The willingness of the person being delivered to be free
5. The knowledge of the Word of God and your level of hatred for sin
6. SELF-DISCIPLINE IS NECESSARY

Also, remember that bondage can be weak or strong. A weak hold can be broken quickly, whereas a stronghold may take a more time. You will not realize the strength of bondage until you faithfully and persistently work on it. You must remember that a foothold can graduate to a stronghold if left unaddressed. After this exercise, set aside some days (with fasting). DO NOT CONTINUE TO DO THE THINGS THAT CAUSED THE "it"! CHANGE YOUR HABITS TO AGREE WITH YOUR PRAYERS. AMEN.

Appendix 2

Exposing the Doors to Bondage

Part I: The bondage

1. When did this bondage start?

2. Was there any unusual things that took place (or you did) when this bondage started?

3. If this bondage started when you were a child: Do you have ancestors who have suffered from a similar kind of bondage?

4. What kind of bondage are you facing? (Fears, depression, voices in your mind, mental illness, physical illness, mental torment, spiritual torment, etc... Please be as detailed as possible.)

5. What are all the things that have impacted your life? (Parent's death, trauma, a certain situation that changed your life, anything that 'changed' you.)

Part II: Your ancestor's background

1. Do you have ancestors who have struggled with similar problems or bondages?

2. Did your bondage start as a child and appear to have no reason to be there?

3. Do you have siblings who suffer from similar bondages or oppression?

Part III: Soul ties

1. Have you been involved with extramarital sex? Are you attracted to an ex-lover? Is he or she a good/godly influence for you?

2. Have you been divorced?

3. Do you feel an unusual attraction to a past boyfriend, girlfriend or lover (who is obviously not right for you)?

4. Do you let anybody dominate, control, or make your choices you?

5. Have you ever formed a blood covenant with another person? (Blood brothers, etc.)

6. Have you ever made vows or agreements with somebody in effort to strengthen the relationship or commit yourself to each other?

7. Do you see any ungodly relationships in your past where gifts were exchanged? (Are you holding onto something that was given to you from somebody you had adultery with, etc.)

8. Have you ever had ungodly relations with any one?

9. Do you have any pictures in your possession of somebody whom you may have an ungodly soul tie with? (A picture of you with somebody you had an adultery with, etc.)

Part IV: Relationship with parents

1. What do you think of your parents?

2. How would you explain your childhood?

3. Where you close to your parents while growing up? If not, why?

4. How would you explain your relationship with your parents? Was it good, bad or very cold?

5. Did you feel rejection from your parents?

6. Was either of your parents overly passive or controlling?

7. Has either of your parents been divorced? Remarried? Are your parents divorced?

8. How would you describe your relationship with your siblings growing up?

Part V: Rejection and abuse

1. Were your parents married when you were conceived? Were you the right sex? Did your parents not want you, or want you to be different (gender, etc.) in any way? If so, explain.

2. Did you feel rejected as a child? As an adult? If so, by whom? Explain.

3. Did you face abuse? What kind (emotional, physical, sexual, etc.) and by whom?

4. Have you faced rejection from your peers, classmates, friends or those around you?

5. Have you ever been put down, belittled, or made fun of? If so, by whom? Explain.

6. If you have faced rejection or abuse, how did you respond? Do you feel you are still paying a price for it? If so, how?

7. How do you respond to rejection right now?

8. Do you reject yourself (self-rejection)? If so, why and in what ways?

Part VI: Unforgiveness or bitterness

1. Is there anybody you feel edgy around? (Don't like them, feel anything in your heart against them, etc.)

2. Do you have anything against anybody? In other words, is there anybody that you have a hard time demonstrating the love of Christ to?

3. Has anybody wronged you that you haven't forgiven from your heart (thoughts, feelings, emotions, etc.)?

4. How do your view your siblings, parents, coworkers, etc.? Do you have any hard feelings against them?

5. Do you make a habit of blaming yourself for everything? Do you obsess over your mistakes and feel unusually guilty for them?

6. Do you deeply regret things that you've done in your past? Could you kick yourself over something you've done in your past? If so, explain.

Part VII: Personality

1. Are you a very positive or negative person?

2. Do you feel confident in yourself? If so, why?

3. Do you have a low self-esteem? If so, why?

4. Are you domineering or controlling? If so, to whom, and in what ways? Why?

5. Are you an achiever? (A go-getter) If so, in what ways?

6. Do you feel that you are always right and that if everybody did everything your way, this world would be a better place to live?

7. How do you treat your children? Husband? Are you controlling, passive, etc.?

8. Do you like people to 'look at you' (as in receive attention)?

Part VIII: Emotional health

1. Do you strive to feel accepted? If so, how does this affect your lifestyle? By whom do you want to feel accepted?

2. Are you always stressed out? If so, why?

3. Do you feel hurt? If so, by whom/what and why?

4. Do you feel good about yourself? If not, why?

5. Do you feel depressed? If so, why? When did it start? Did your parents or grandparents struggle with depression? If so, then do you know when it started and why? Do you have siblings who are also struggling? Do you feel your depression is rational or irrational?

6. Do you struggle with fears? If so, what is it that you fear? (Fear of heights, dying, being hopeless, failure, never marrying, etc.)

7. Do you worry about things? What things do you worry about? Why?

8. Do you struggle with anger? Do you have a short temper?

9. Do you have any insecurity? If so, explain.

10. Do you feel any self-pity or feel sorry for yourself? Have you ever felt this? If so, why?

11. Do you find it easy to hate people? If so, over what kinds of things would a person have to do to make you hate them?

12. Do you have any irrational feelings? If so, what are they?

13. Do you feel like something is wrong with you?

14. Do you feel excessively guilty over anything? Is this a continual problem?

15. Are you very confused and forgetful? (Beyond the normal)

16. Are you aware of any emotional wounds that have affected you?

17. Have you ever been deeply embarrassed over something? What was it?

18. Have you been in or are currently experiencing very difficult (depressing) circumstances which may cause you to feel hopeless or depressed?

Part IX: Who are you in Christ? And how do you see God?

1. How do you explain your relationship with God?

2. Do you feel you aren't good enough to meet His standards?

3. Do you see Him as a loving father, or a dictator?

4. Do you believe that it's only by the Blood of Jesus that your sins are forgiven? Or do you feel you need to earn your forgiveness in any way?

5. Do you feel God's love in your life?

6. Do you feel like your sins are forgiven? Or do you feel guilty?

7. Do you feel excessively guilty in everyday life?

8. Do you feel that doing good things, you earn God's love and acceptance?

9. Do you feel that God is angry or upset with you?

Part X: Spoken curses, vows & oaths

1. Have you ever spoken something negative about yourself that has come to past? For example: "I'm sick and tired..." or "If I don't quit typing, I'm going to get arthritis!"

2. Has your parents, or those in authority over you spoken out a curse over you? For example: "You'll never amount to anything!" or "You'll never get out of debt" or "You're so dumb"

3. Have you ever made a vow out of anger? If so, what? For example: "I'll never let anybody push me around again!" or "I'm never going to be hurt again!"

4. Have you ever wished to die? Have you ever said it?

5. If you have made any vows or oaths, what are they?

Part XI: Relationships

1. Do you have many friends? What kind of people are they?

2. Do you have a hard time trying to meet new people or make friends?

3. Are you socially outgoing or shy? If so, why?

4. How would you define your relationship with your spouse?

Part XII: Sexuality

1. Have you ever had unholy sex? What kind? (Fornication, adultery, sodomy, with a child, etc.)

2. Have you struggled with lust, fantasy or unholy sexual thoughts? If so, what kind?

3. Have you been attracted to pornography?

4. Do you have homosexual thoughts and desires? If so, have you acted upon those feelings?

5. How do you feel about your sexuality? (Do you feel dirty about it, or do you feel it's a wonderful blessing that God's given you?)

6. Do you withhold sex from your spouse or are you fidgety? Do you enjoy a healthy relationship with your spouse sexually? How does he or she react?

7. Have you ever been raped or sexually abused?

8. Have you ever woke up and felt a sexual presence with you? There are demons that imitate male and female functions, and stimulate their host (a person) sexually (beyond the normal 'wet dream').

9. Do you struggle or have you struggled with masturbation?

10. Do you struggle or have you struggled with any other sexual related thoughts, desires, or bondages?

11. Is there anything sexually that you are ashamed of?

Part XIII: Addictions

1. Do you have any addictions? If so, what kind? (Drugs, alcohol, smoking, eating, sex, TV, etc.) When did they start?

2. Did anybody else in your family (siblings, ancestors, etc.) have a struggle with any addictions? If so, what? Who?

3. Have you ever had, or currently have any sort of obsession over anything? If so, what?

Part XIV: False religions

Examples of false religions: Buddhism, Hindu, Jehovah Witness, Mormonism, Christian Scientists, eastern religions, etc.

1. Have you ever been involved with any false religions? If so, why, when and how long? How do you feel about those beliefs now?

2. Have you ever been involved in any secret societies such as Freemasonry? If so, how deep were you involved?

Part XV: The occult

1. Have you ever shown interest in the occult? If so, in what ways? (Read up on it, dabbled in it, etc.)

2. Do you still feel drawn or attracted to the occult?

3. Have you had any interest in horror or thriller style movies or novels? Are you still attracted to these things?

4. Have you ever made a vow with the devil? If so, what?

5. Married Satan?

6. Worshipped a demon or Satan?

7. Have you ever put a curse or spell on somebody?

8. Are you aware of any curses or spells placed on you? If so, what? Who did it?

9. Dabbled with an Ouija board? If so, why?

10. Ever been a member of a coven (group of 13 witches)? Explain.

11. Communicated with the dead? Explain.

12. Told somebody's fortune or went to see a fortune teller? Explain.

13. Ever read your horoscope?

14. Watched or been involved in a séance? Explain.

15. Have you been involved or a victim of Satanic Ritual Abuse (SRA)? Explain.

16. Been baptized into a false religion or any other evil baptism? If so, what were you baptized into? When?

17. Have you ever had a spirit guide?

18. Have you ever been involved with meditation, yoga, karate, or related activities?

19. Were you or anybody in your family superstitious? If so, who?

20. Ever been involved in astral travel? (Out of body)

21. If you have made any vows or oaths, what are they? Were there any sacrifices or rituals that were accompanied with them?

22. Have you ever made a blood pact before? If so, with whom (including persons, demons and Satan) and for what purpose?

23. Have you ever partaken in automatic writing, automatic drawing or automatic painting?

24. Have you ever been involved in Yoga, transcendental meditation, or similar activities?

25. Have you ever sought healing from a spiritual source other than Jesus Christ? (New age healing, energy healing, etc.)

26. Any other involvement in the occult? Explain.

Part XVI: Un-confessed sins

1. Are there any un-confessed sins that you have not repented of? (Usually something you've done, that you know is wrong, but won't admit to it. An abortion, stealing, etc. are some examples.)

2. Is there anything you've been hiding inside that you haven't confessed?

3. Do you feel excessively guilty over something(s) you've done in the past? If so, what?

Part XVII: Cursed objects

1. Do you have any idols, occult rings, or anything that could hold evil spiritual value in your home? If so, what? Any objects that hold evil spiritual value must be destroyed.

2. Do you have any gifts saved from sinful relationships? If so, explain. For example, if a man gives a woman a personal gift during an adultery that needs to be sold or destroyed.

Part XVIII: Severe trauma, abuse & disassociation

1. Have you ever been exposed to extreme abuse or a traumatic experience? Did it have a drastic effect on your emotional or mental system? If so, what happen? How did it affect you?

2. Have you ever disassociated or been diagnosed with Dissociative Identity Disorder (DID) or Multiple Personality Disorder (MPD)?

3. Are you aware of any alters (other personalities) that you may have? (If so, tell me about them)

4. Do you have a memory gap where you cannot remember a certain time of your life?

5. Do you have false memories of things that really didn't take place?

6. Have you ever been in a car accident or other traumatic situation? Have you ever witnessed a tragedy in real life?

Part XIX: Weaknesses

1. Do you struggle with any habitual sins? If so, what? Do you want to break those bad habits?

2. Do you struggle with any weaknesses such as lust, anger, hate, etc.? If so, what? Do you know where they came from or how they got started? Do you want to break free from those weaknesses?

Part XX: Pregnancy issues

1. Have you ever said something along the lines of, "I will never have children"?

2. Have you ever had an abortion or attempted one?

3. Have you ever had incest or ungodly sexual relations with somebody related to you? (See Leviticus 20:19-21, as this can cause a curse to land upon you which needs to be broken)

Part XXI: Other things to look for

1. Have you ever tried drugs? If so, how much, and how did it affect you? Why did you try drugs?

2. Have you ever thought about or attempted suicide?

3. Do you have any physical or mental disabilities, diseases or illnesses? Explain.

4. Do you want, and are willing to be delivered? Are you willing to give up those demon spirits and maybe make some lifestyle changes in order to keep your deliverance?

5. Do you experience unusual confusion settle upon you as you try to pray and read the Bible?

6. What kind of music do you like? (Please list all styles of music you currently enjoy, and give examples in each category you list, such as some names of artists and songs)

7. Have you previously enjoyed hard rock, metal, acid, alternative, rap, new age, or any other kind of worldly music? (Please provide some examples of artists and songs from each genre (type/style) of music you list)

8. Have you had any nightmares or weird experiences at night while supposedly sleeping?

9. Have you ever been in a trance or had an out of body experience?

10. Have you ever noticed time slipped right out from under you? For example, you look at your watch and its 7:00pm, then you look again what seemed like 15 minutes later and its 2:00am. This is a sign of a trance.

11. Have you ever touched or kissed a dead body? If so, explain whom and why and what happened afterwards.

12. Do you feel that you somehow have to earn your forgiveness? Do you 'wonder' if your sins are truly forgiven -- all of them? Are you aware of any signs of legalism or religious spirits operating in your mind?

13. Do you have any physical infirmities, sickness or diseases? If so, please list them.

14. Are you on any medications? If so, please explain.

15. Are you entertained by movies or TV shows which glorify death, murder, pain or suffering of others? Please explain.

16. Have you ever had any other kind of weird encounter with the spiritual realm?

Use this information to expose the root cause of the "it".

REFERENCES

1. Gary R. Collins, *Christian Counseling: A Comprehensive Guide*, 3rd Addition, Revised and Updated, NavPress, Colorado Springs, Colorado. ISBN 1418503290
2. Beilby, J.K. & P.R. Eddy. *Understanding Spiritual Warfare: Four Views*. Grand Rapids, Michigan: Baker, 2012.
3. Boyd, G.A., *God at War: The Bible and Spiritual Conflict*. Downers Grove, Illinois: IVP, 1997.
4. Hiebert, P. "Spiritual Warfare and Worldview"
5. Stedman, R.C, *Spiritual Warfare: Winning the Daily Battle with Satan.* Portland, Oregon: Multnomah, 1975.
6. Pirolo, N., *Prepare for Battle: Basic Training in Spiritual Warfare*, San Diego, California: Emmaus Road, International, 1997.
7. Arnold, E. C., *3 Crucial Questions about Spiritual Warfare*, Grand Rapids, Michigan: Baker, 1997.l
8. Rita Bennett, You Can Be Emotionally Free, 1982 ISBN 978 0 88270 748 8
9. Rita Bennett, Emotionally Free, 1982, ISBN 0 86065 194 0
   Publishers, PO Box 777,
10. Tonbridge, Kent TN 11 0ZS, England, 1997, reprinted 2004). ISBN 1-85240-110-9. (Available in the US through the Arsenal Bookstore, 11005 Voyager Parkway, Colorado Springs, CO 80921.)
11. John and Paula Sandford, Healing the Wounded Spirit (Victory House, 1985). ISBN 0-932081-14-2.
12. Norma Dearing, The Healing Touch (Chosen Books, 2002). ISBN 0-8007-9302-1. Charles Kraft, Deep Wounds, Deep Healing (Servant Pub., 1993). ISBN 0-89283-784-5.
13. Derek Prince, God's Remedy for Rejection (Whitaker House, 1993). ISBN 088368-864-6.
14. Francis and Judith MacNutt, Praying for Your Unborn Child (1989). ISBN 0-38523-2829. (Available from www.Christianhealingmin.org, 904-765-3332.)
15. Thomas Verney, MD, The Secret Life of the Unborn Child (Summit Books, 1981).
16. Anderson, Winning Spiritual Warfare 1990 ISBN 13: 978-0-89081-868-8 James
17. Friesen, Uncovering the Mystery of MPD, 1997 ISBN 1-56819-062-7
18. Diane Hawkins, Multiple Identities, 2009 ISBN 978-0-9708073-6-6,
19. Restoration in Christ Ministries, http://www.rcm-usa.org/index.htm
20. Francis MacNutt, Deliverance from Evil Spirits, 1995, 0-8007-9232-7, Chap 17, pp 223-235 (best introductory material)
21. Daniel Ryder, Breaking the Circle of SRA, 1992, 0-89638-258-3 (an excellent book by a Christian counselor)
22. Margaret Smith, Ritual Abuse, what it is, why it happens, how to help, 1993, 0-06-250214-X (in depth information about SRA and MPD)
23. The Christian Bible
24. The following associations focus on trauma and disassociation www.sidran.org, www.issd.org
25. Pentecost, J.D., *Your Adversary the Devil.* Grand Rapids, Michigan: Zondervan, 1969

About the Author
Dr. Paulette Douglas

Dr. Paulette Douglas truly epitomizes elegance in living a saved, sanctified and Holy life, set apart from the secular world! Dr. Douglas is an ordained minister with the Pentecostal Assemblies of the World, an anointed national and international Evangelist, teacher and preacher. Dr. Paulette Douglas is renowned for the ministry of exhortation to the Body of Christ through deliverance, inner healing, salvation and biblical counseling at seminars, prayer clinics, crusades and conferences. She has established three churches and assisted in establishing many other churches, ministries and colleges as she serves on the Body of Christ for Jesus. Dr. Douglas was baptized in the name of Jesus Christ and filled with the Holy Ghost in 1977. She was called to the ministry in 1981, taught bible study at Pacific Bell for nine years which established the Radiant Life in Christ Ministries. She was the founder and pastor of the Radiant Life in Christ Community Church in Baldwin Park, California for nearly four years. Dr. Douglas retired in 1996 with full benefits from AT&T after 26 years of service. God introduced Dr. Douglas to the LOVE and HERO of her life, Bishop Robert T. Douglas Sr. They were married, the ministries merged, and she became the First Lady of the Jacob's Ladder Family, the Women's Ministry Director, the Church Executive Administrator and the Dean of the California University of Theology. Dr. Robert and Paulette Douglas are the proud parents of three wonderful children, Shakinah, Robert Jr. and Sondra Imani. They are also blessed with two granddaughters, Demi and Rob'Ann (butter ball) four grandsons, Dylan, Dominick Terrell, the twins Canden and Caden. Seven Godchildren and twelve God -grandchildren. Dr. Douglas is a graduate from Fuller Theological Seminary, Pasadena, California, Pentecostal Bible College, Ministerial Training Institute of Inglewood, California and Aenon Bible College West Coast. She has a Bachelors degree in Biblical Studies, a Masters degree in Theology, a PhD in Theology, Administration and a PhD in Biblical Counseling. She has earned certificates from California Christian Leadership of Orange County in biblical counseling, Zoe Christian Leadership Training Institute, Church Growth International, Seoul Korea and School of World Missions and Evangelism, Los Angeles. Dr. Douglas is formerly the Dean/Professor of the Inglewood Ministerial Training Institute of Inglewood, the Inland Empire Ministerial Training Institute, the Tri-County Ministerial Training Institute (San Bernardino, Riverside and Los Angeles counties) and the Living Waters Bible College, Rialto California. Dr. Douglas is presently the Dean of Colleges and Professor for the California District Council Aenon Bible College and Institutes, the Jacob's Ladder California University of Theology and Aenon Bible Institute CDC Extension Campus in Inglewood, California and the American College Theological Seminary International University (ACTS). All schools are fully accredited institutions for pastors, evangelist, teachers and anyone who has the call of God on their lives for ministry. Dr. Douglas is currently the CDC International Missions President and the past Church/Extension/Evangelism/Altar Director for the California District Council of the Pentecostal Assemblies of the World, Inc. Past Evangelism President for the CHDC Area 2 and has worked with the PAW Evangelism Ministry for more than 35 years. Dr. Paulette Douglas is the published author of the book series "Get Rid of It before It Gets Rid of You". Self-Help Instructions on how to correct and receive deliverance in every area of your life. Dr. Douglas portrays tremendous strength and endurance in the Lord by jointly sharing the vision and love for God with Bishop Douglas. Her primary objective in life is to be that "Excellent Woman of God, walking in His Divine favor.

Books and Recourses Compiled by
Dr. Paulette Douglas

"How to Get Rid of "it", Before "it" Gets Rid of You" Series (12 Books on Self Deliverance)

Volume One- Healing and Deliverance from Additions

Volume Two- Healing and Deliverance from Sexual Additions

Volume Three- Healing and Deliverance from Personality Disorders

Volume Four- Healing and Deliverance from Negative Relationships

Volume Five- Healing and Deliverance Through Spiritual Warfare

Volume Six- Healing and Deliverance from Negatives Attitudes

Volume Seven- Healing and Deliverance from Success Hindrances

Volume Eight- Healing and Deliverance from Tormenting Emotions

Volume Nine- Healing and Deliverance from Spiritual Weakness

Volume Ten- Healing and Deliverance from Salvation Issues

Volume Eleven- Healing and Deliverance from Domestic Problems

Volume Twelve- Healing and Deliverance Through Biblical Counseling

How to Have an Anointed Altar Workers Ministry

How to Have an Effective Prayer and Fasting Life

How to Walk in Your Grace as the Wife of a Minister, Deacon, Pastor, or Bishop

How to be an Effective Life Coach